Field Guide

GESTURES

How to Identify and Interpret Virtually Every Gesture Known to Man

By Nancy Armstrong and Melissa Wagner

QUIRK BOOKS

PHILADELPHIA

DISCLAIMER

There are millions of gestures in the world and even more interpretations. While every care has been taken to represent the most popular gestures and to explain their meanings worldwide, the authors and publisher cannot guarantee that this guide addresses every variation of meaning or every gesture in the world.

Library of Congress Cataloging in Publication Number: 2002094026

ISBN: 1-931686-20-3

Printed in Singapore

Typeset in Adobe Garamond, Franklin Gothic, and Impact

Designed by Andrea Leigh Stephany
Illustrations by Judy Francis
Photography by William Drake (www.PhotoDrake.com)

All photographs copyright © 2003 by Quirk Productions, Inc.

Distributed in North America by Chronicle Books
85 Second Street
San Francisco, CA 94105

10 9 8 7 6 5 4 3 2

Quirk Books
215 Church Street
Philadelphia, PA 19106
www.quirkbooks.com

Contents

Field Guide to Gestures

V. OFFENSIVE AND PROFANE

VI. JUST FOR EMPHASIS

VII. NO WORDS NEEDED

Introduction

"It is gestures that use us as their instruments, as their bearers and incarnations."—Milan Kundera, *Immortality*

Gestures are fascinating things, at once wholly expressive and curiously mysterious. The flick of the wrist, the wave of a finger, or simply the movement of an eyelid can say more than a speech, and sometimes a subtle gesture can express a feeling more gracefully than words.

In this book, you will find out all there is to know about more than 100 gestures—from the hand purse to the horns to the point to the finger. *Field Guide to Gestures* invites you to explore the origins, uses, regional variations (in both meaning and performance), and environments where you would most often experience each gesture.

Confused by someone's gesture? Refer to the color plates to find an example of the gesture in use. Then locate the gesture in one of the seven categories—Arrival/Departure, Approval, Disapproval, Mating, Offensive and Profane, Just for Emphasis, or No Words Needed—for a full description to shed light on your situation.

Field Guide to Gestures tells you when and where to avoid using particular gestures, where you'll have the most success using each gesture, and how each gesture came to be. The step-by-step execution directions, with instructional line drawings, will help you incorporate the gesture into your body language lexicon.

Next time you're out and about and come across an unfamiliar gesture, refer to *Field Guide to Gestures* and you'll quickly learn what friends, coworkers, and passersby are *really* saying when they communicate nonverbally.

I. Arrival and Departure

1. 📷 **BLOWN KISS**

Usage and
Origins:

The fingers of one hand are brought to the lips, lightly kissed, turned palm up in front of the mouth, and blown on, as though launching the kiss into the air. Blowing a kiss is a way to send love and good wishes from a distance; it could be an enforced distance, such as across the gangway, or a space kept by those playing hard to get. In common, everyday use, the blown kiss gesture is a way to say goodbye.

While anthropologists have been unable to concretely explain the origins of the kiss, it is clear that the blown kiss gesture evolved from the actual act of kissing. (For more on the kiss itself, see page 19.) While this long-distance kiss gesture is not as intimate or tender as a lip-to-lip or lip-to-cheek kiss, similar affection is certainly conveyed.

Region:

This gesture is popular throughout North America and Europe, where it is generally understood as affectionate but inoffensive.

Avoid blowing kisses in Islamic areas of the Middle East and Africa, where laws against public displays of affection are strict.

Environment: Parades are a common venue for kiss-blowing, as beauty queens and other participants will use this gesture to greet onlookers. In black-and-white films, you will often see this gesture as lovers part tearfully on a crowded train platform, and celebratory cruisers can be seen blowing kisses into the crowd amassed to wish a bon voyage.

A blown kiss gesture can certainly also have a come-hither feel. The flirtatious kiss blown across a boisterous party or jam-packed bar leaves little room for interpretation; the kiss-blower has love on his mind and hope in his heart. A person on a subway platform might catch a glimpse of someone blowing a kiss as the train roars away; this might be considered a "lost opportunity."

Execution: 1. Face the person to whom you would like to blow a kiss.

2. Bring your fingertips to your lips, holding the rest of your hand flat.

3. Kiss the tips of your fingers.

4. Rotate your wrist back to bring your fingers away from your mouth and to orient your palm straight up. Your hand should make an angle of between 45 and 90 degrees with your forearm.

5. **If you are blowing the kiss toward a specific person, make eye contact.**

6. **Blow across the palm of your hand, aiming your fingertips in the direction of the other person.**

Variations of Performance:

If you are blowing a kiss to a large crowd of people, it is acceptable to sweep the hand used away from your body dramatically and arc the entire arm over the group.

For the enthusiastic, and those blowing a kiss to the multitudes, you might bring both hands to your mouth simultaneously, kiss the fingertips of both hands at the same time, and then flamboyantly extend your arms out to either side.

2.   **THE BOW**

Usage and Origins:

The body is bent forward at the waist. Bowing is a submissive gesture that shows the utmost respect and humility toward the figure to whom one bows. During the fifteenth century, both men and women employed a bowing curtsey as a formal greeting; over time, the gesture became two gestures: the bow for men and the curtsey for women. These days in the West, bowing to show respect is primarily reserved for royalty, but even in this case convention dictates that it is not always necessary. For instance, if you're not a British citizen you needn't bow before the Queen, but it's a good idea to do so if you are.

Around the world, the bow gesture can also be observed in the theater, where it has been a standard gesture for centuries, performed by both actors and actresses at the end of a show as a humble thanks to an appreciative audience. The phrase "break a leg" originated as a reference to the bow—it comes from seventeenth-century English, in which "break" meant "bend." Thus, to encourage someone to break a leg actually meant that you hoped he would be asked to bow to the audience after a good performance. The phrase survives today, but it is unlikely that most users equate its meaning with much more than "good luck."

In Japan, bowing is the standard greeting: The depth and length of the bow indicate separate meanings. Generally, there are three types of bows in Japan: An informal 15-degree bow, a formal 30-degree bow, and a bow of greater than 30 degrees, which is strictly reserved for the imperial Japanese family. The rules of thumb are: When bowing to a person of high status, the 30-degree bow is required. If a person is bowing to you and they are of lower rank, make certain they bow first, and for a bit longer. The Japanese are very serious about the etiquette of the bow gesture—it is considered rude and improper even for a visiting Westerner to bow deeply to a person who is of lower status, despite the best intentions.

Region: The bow is a gesture that is seen in theaters the world over, from Katmandu to Kansas City.

As a greeting, it is less common but will be seen in Asian countries and in Germany, where ordinary folk can still be seen bowing to say hello.

In the United States, you will rarely see this gesture outside the theater. In countries where sovereigns reign, this gesture is much more common, as it is still employed as a show of respect to royalty in most aristocracies.

Environment: A street corner in Germany, a conference room in Japan, a high-school auditorium in Poughkeepsie, and a glamorous Broadway theater are all likely places to witness the bow gesture.

If used facetiously, as if to say "Your wish is my command" to someone who is being bossy, this gesture might be practiced in private homes, or anywhere a friend or spouse might decide to bark orders.

Execution: 1. **Stand straight and tall, feet together and shoulders back.**

2. Clasp your hands behind your back or rest your palms flat against the sides of your thighs.

3. With your eyes lowered, bend forward at the waist. Lower your torso as far as is appropriate.

4. Straighten.

Variations of Performance:

The curtsey, or the "woman's bow," is commonly known as a variant of bowing, since in the past the two were used together in the same gesture. The curtsey is, however, actually a variation of kneeling that in previous centuries was performed by both men and women. You'll rarely see a man or a woman curtsey these days, but it is performed as follows: Position your feet so that your heels are together and your toes are pointed outward, then bend your knees slightly. For more of a flourish, bring one leg behind the other before bending them. This gesture is often accompanied by a slight lift of the skirt worn by the woman performing the curtsey.

The *namaste* is an Indian greeting wherein the hands are pressed with palms together as if in prayer, accompanied by a slight bow. It is used the way Westerners use the handshake gesture (see HANDSHAKE, page 10), and can also mean "thank you" or "I'm sorry." The same gesture, conveying the same meaning, is also used in Thailand and is called the *wai*.

3.   **FIST-CHEST POUND**

Usage and
Origins:

The hand, in the shape of a fist, pounds the chest in the
area where the heart is located, then forms a peace sign.
The fist-chest pound gesture, which roughly translates to "peace out," is mainly used as a farewell signal
in cities by youths and those wanting to appear
extremely cool. The pounding of the chest indicates
that those being gestured to are close to the gesturer's
heart, and the peace sign is a symbol of well-wishing.

This gesture should be attempted only if the user
is certain he or she can pull it off without seeming
false. Those in suburban areas who have the urge to
perform this hip gesture are advised that it has not
yet become widely accepted outside urban environments.

Region:

The fist-chest pound gesture will be recognized and
reciprocated in large cities throughout the United
States, and perhaps in some bustling European cities
as well.

Environment:

This form of farewell is solely appropriate in an
urban environment; a busy street corner, a crowded
subway platform, or by a kiosk are all places where
you might see two friends use the fist-chest pound
gesture as they take their leave.

Execution: 1. Make a fist with your right hand [Fig. A].

2. Bring the fist to your chest, near the heart, palm facing your body.

3. Strike your chest twice, rapidly. A soft thudding sound should be audible.

4. After the second pound, extend your index and middle finger into a "V" [Fig. B]. Often the hand and arm are still angled across the body, and the top of the "V" points to the upper left.

5. Drop your hand.

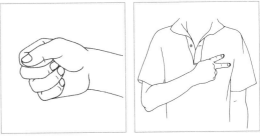

Fig. A   Fig. B

Variations of Performance:
The peace sign can be flashed without the chest pound. (For more on this gesture, see THE "V," page 227.)

4. **HANDSHAKE**

Usage and Origins:
Two people grasp hands and pump. The handshake is a gesture that existed as early as the sixteenth century. The handshake gesture was originally used to bind a contract, and it was often accompanied by kneeling on the part of the subordinate party in the agreement. At that time, it was important to know whether a hand held a weapon, and shaking hands was a symbolic way to determine this.

For centuries, the handshake was not an appropriate greeting—it was unacceptable for someone of a lower rank to mirror the gesture of someone of higher status. However, in the early nineteenth century, as many Western countries embraced democracy, the gesture became widely used between people of all ranks and status.

Presently, the handshake gesture is used as a greeting, to show the acceptance of a contract, and to wish someone congratulations. It is one of the most popular gestures in existence.

Region: The handshake exists all over the world, but there are nuances of the gesture in various lands that affect the meaning. In the United States, where aggressiveness in business and life are considered virtues, a firm grip along with direct eye contact is expected.

Conversely, in Asian countries such as Japan and Korea, eye contact is considered too aggressive, and the grip should be gentle to convey respect.

In Northern Europe and in business situations in North America, it is common for women to extend a hand for shaking. In Islamic countries, men are not allowed to touch women they are not closely related to, so inter-sex handshakes are taboo in these regions.

In most of Southern Europe and Central and South America, handshakes are warmer and last longer, and the hand that is not doing the shaking is often employed to touch the hand, arm, shoulder, or lapel of the other person. In Russia, a handshake is often accompanied by a hug.

The handshake gesture is recognized around the globe, but in certain areas, traditional greetings that have similar meanings are still preferred. For example, in India, the *namaste* is used, with hands pressed, palms together, as in prayer, and a slight bow (see THE BOW, page 4). In Thailand, the same gesture is used, but it is called the *wai* (see THE BOW, page 4.)

In Arab countries, the more formal *salaam* is used as a greeting: the hand touches the chest, then lips, then forehead and ends with the hand raised, palm out, and the head bowed. It means "I give you my heart, my soul, and my head."

In Japan, bowing is used in place of a handshake (See THE BOW, page 4).

Environment: From high-rise business towers to stadiums to backyard barbecues, the handshake is a gesture that is not confined to one milieu.

Execution: The handshake is a gesture that involves two people.

1. Approach another person, usually someone you have not seen for some time, have never met, or wish to congratulate.

2. Form a paddle with your right hand, pressing your fingers close together. The thumb extends straight up.

3. Extend your right hand at hip level.

4. Meet the outstretched right hand of the other person with your right hand, palm-to-palm. The hands come together at the joint of the thumb and index finger.

5. Once the palms meet, wrap your fingers around the outside of the other person's hand.

6. Squeeze the other hand. The firmness with which you squeeze will depend on cultural norms.

7. Pump the arm and hand up and down at least once. A typical enthusiastic greeting will express itself in multiple pumpings.

8. The hands then separate, and conversation typically ensues.

Variations of Performance: Friendly but formal is the idea behind the "politician's handshake," wherein the left hand covers the top of the shaking hands. This is meant to convey closeness and sincerity.

5. 📷 **HANG LOOSE**

Usage and Origins: *The pinkie and thumb are extended from a fist as the forearm twists, causing the hand to wiggle back and forth.* This gesture, in modern usage, loosely translates to "relax" or "be cool," and is most commonly associated with surfers of the Hawaiian islands. Its origins can be traced to Spanish explorers and immigrants from the Spanish colonies of the Americas.

As the Spaniards arrived on the Hawaiian Islands, they showed their friendly intentions to the local residents by flashing a gesture which, to the Spaniards, meant "Let's share a drink"—the thumb and pinkie fingers were splayed out from a fist, with the thumb raised to the lips and the hand twisted back and forth, as if miming the action of drinking. (For more on the Spanish drinking gesture, see LET'S DRINK, page 213.)

Over time, this drinking gesture evolved into what is now referred to as the hang loose gesture, with the hand moving away from the lips and into the air. In contemporary times, the gesture has lost its initial meaning as an invitation to drink, and its Spanish origin is unknown to most Hawaiian islanders. In Hawaii, you may hear residents refer to the gesture as the "shaka" gesture, named so because of its use by a well-known television personality who flashes the gesture while saying the words, "It's a shaka!" meaning "It's a shocker."

Though the gesture has gained popularity outside of the islands via the growth of surfing culture, it remains largely a "niche gesture." This does not mean, however, that non-surfers must steer clear of it, since the signal itself is very laid-back and inclusive.

This gesture will primarily be used as a greeting, a goodbye, or to share excitement when swells on the North Shore are particularly perfect.

Region:　Though its use began in Hawaii, this gesture is used throughout the United States as a "cool" way to say goodbye, usually to friends.

　　In Mexico, the hang loose gesture has a different meaning altogether—it is done vertically as opposed to horizontally, resembling the handle on a stein of beer, and is a way to ask someone if they'd like a drink. (See LET'S DRINK, page 213.)

　　It means "six" in Japan, when counting using one's fingers or when indicating the number to someone, as when placing an order at a store or requesting a table at a restaurant.

Environment:　A sunny beach is the perfect spot to see a tan hand flash this gesture, though due to the permeation of surf culture into non-beach areas, you might notice former hippies and college students gesturing to each other to "hang loose" on the quad, in a city, or at the mall on the West Coast of the United States.

Execution:　1. **Make a loose fist.**

　　2. **Extend the pinkie and the thumb to either side.**

　　3. **Shake the hand lightly, using the forearm as the axis of rotation** [FIG. A].

Fig. A

---

6. **HUG**

Usage and
Origins:

The arms are wrapped around the torso of a companion; usually, the action is reciprocated. The hug gesture is a personal, informal gesture of greeting used when parting or reuniting to show warmth and affection. Historians postulate that the embrace as greeting originated in the Middle Ages to ensure that no weapons were concealed under a potential combatant's robes. Today it has become a social convention devoid of such associations.

　　Hugs are given and received upon arrival and departure, but they are also multi-faceted gestures that help fulfill the desire for close human contact. Hugs can express comfort, joy, and even passion. A mother hugs her son to relieve his pain, friends share an embrace at the mention of bad news, a player hugs a teammate after a hard game is won, and a client hugs an attorney when she has been acquitted. Lovers may share an extended embrace at the initiation of a sexual exchange.

The duration and intensity of a hug will be determined by the relationship of those embracing as well as the situation that evokes the embrace. At its simplest, a hug conveys tender feelings of love, comfort, and familiarity.

Region: Embracing standards vary across cultures. In Latin America, the *abrazo*, a long, intense hug followed by several claps on the back, is the norm, while hugs in Asian cultures are more reserved, giving just a quick squeeze. People in Islamic countries do not perform public displays of affection with members of the opposite sex because of strict laws governing public touching. Most North Americans and Europeans find this intimate form of contact with strangers uncomfortable and keep hugging to a minimum apart from family and close friends.

Environment: Any locale where people leave or are reunited with one another is a good place to see the hug gesture in action—airports, train stations, and even restaurants and bars see their share of hugging. Since hugs are employed at times of heartbreak and celebration alike, funerals and weddings are common events where embraces can be observed. However, as an event is not a prerequisite for a hug, you are just as likely to experience one in your bedroom or kitchen as anywhere else.

Execution: The hug is a gesture that involves two people.

1. Raise both arms as you approach another person. The other person will do the same.

2. Offset your arms so that your right arm is up toward the other person's left shoulder and your left arm is down toward the other person's waist. The other person will do the same.

3. As your bodies come into contact, wrap your arms around the torso of the other person.

4. Squeeze once.

5. Release.

Variations of Performance: Putting your arm around another person is a kind of half-hug, and can be seen when lovers put their arms around each other's waists or shoulders with their sides pressed together (see Arm Around, page 89).

7. **KISS**

Usage and Origins:

Puckered lips touch some part of a companion's body, usually the lips, cheek, hand, or forehead. Experts argue that kissing is derived from the sucking motion of an infant at the breast, or from pre-historic humans, when ancient mothers passed food to their infants in the same manner as birds. From there, it evolved as a gesture of greeting and is prevalent all over the world. In general, kissing can be relegated to two categories, public kissing and private kissing.

Public kissing encompasses the greeting and myriad other uses. In most cultures, kissing on the cheek in greeting is standard, but the style and the level of intimacy it conveys varies. In the United States, for instance, a kiss on the cheek is performed once, quickly, and is generally reserved for relatives.

Hand-kissing is chivalrous though outdated, and these days, it tends to be bestowed only on important figures, such as the Pope or a mob godfather, or in a facetious or flirtatious manner.

Mothers kiss the wounds of children, athletes kiss trophies, the pious kiss religious relics and statues, wanderers kiss the soil upon reaching safe ground, and so forth.

Private kissing involves romance. "French kissing," with mutual tongue contact and mouth exploration, is reserved for personal and amorous relationships and should not be employed in greetings or other non-romantic situations. If a "French kiss" is bestowed on a near-stranger in public, such as at a club, it should be considered an extremely aggressive gesture. One's reaction to it, whether positive or negative, will, of course, depend on mood and circumstance.

Region: The amount of kissing that goes on in a culture varies greatly throughout the world. Among the Tapuya of South America, kisses are exchanged only between males, as a sign of peace. The French are fond of kissing one another at all occasions (so fond, in fact, that they've had a kiss named after them) and even kiss their own fingertips as a sign of appreciation for superb food or drink. As a greeting, the French will most often kiss both cheeks in succession, sometimes returning to the first cheek for a third kiss.

In most countries, public "French kissing" is taboo, and you should be especially cautious when kissing publicly in certain Islamic countries such as Saudi Arabia, where laws regarding public displays of affection are strict.

Environment: A kiss on the cheek or even a quick peck on the lips can be seen everywhere, from street corners to cocktail parties. "French kissing," however, is best confined to private spaces—to do otherwise is sure to offend observers and perhaps even the person you are kissing.

Execution: Kissing is a gesture that involves two people.

1. Purse, or pucker, the lips.

2. Lean in toward another person's face. Closing your eyes is optional.

3. When your lips meet the other person's lips, press together and push against the other person lightly.

4. After a short time, release the pressure between your lips as you draw away from the other person's mouth. In some cases, a "smacking" sound will be audible.

Variations of Performance: In one version of the kiss, you may advance toward the other person, turn your head slightly away from his or her mouth, and deliver the kiss to the cheek. The smacking sound should be audible.

In another, instead of planting your lips squarely on the cheek of another person, press most of your cheek against the other person's cheek. Even if you do not make any physical contact with your lips, be sure the smacking sound is heard. These kisses are often called "air kisses" and can even be employed without the touching of cheeks at all; the kiss is delivered to the air above the shoulder of the other person, and the other person does the same to the air above your shoulder. Usually this is followed by switching sides, and the air above both shoulders is kissed.

"French kissing" involves opening the mouth and extending your tongue until it touches the tongue of the other person.

8.   **LIVE LONG AND PROSPER**

Usage and Origins:

The palm is held flat and facing out while the middle and ring fingers are splayed apart, with a space in between. This gesture was popularized by the television show *Star Trek*, and is still practiced by enthusiastic fans (often referred to as "Trekkers" or "Trekkies"). Mr. Spock, a half-alien/half-human from the planet Vulcan, was the originator of the gesture on the show. Leonard Nimoy was asked to contrive the gesture for the Vulcan departure. He decided on a gesture he'd seen as a boy in synagogue—a priestly benediction meant to resemble the Hebrew letter "shin," the first letter of "Shadai," a secret name of God. Mr. Spock used this gesture in greeting or farewell, and the phrase "Live long and prosper" was usually spoken while he somberly made the gesture.

During the television show's heyday, many fans employed this gesture commonly. In the twenty-first century, however, the gesture is most often used sarcastically to poke fun at those Trekkies who converge at

Star Trek conventions dressed in costumes, role-play characters from the show, and refer to obscure lines from all of the 79 original episodes. These days, use of this gesture is not widespread, and perhaps the only absolutely safe place to try it out might be at a *Star Trek* convention.

Region: This gesture is not likely to be understood or used outside of English-speaking countries, where *Star Trek* is most well-known.

The gesture can also still be seen in practice in its ancient form, as a benediction performed by a rabbi in Jewish religious gatherings.

Environment: The aforementioned *Star Trek* conventions, which still occur fairly regularly, are the best place to witness this gesture. The most common spot to see the live long and prosper gesture at work and in its true element, however, is still in a vintage episode of the show itself.

Execution: 1. **Raise your right hand to chest-level, palm outward.**

2. **Splay your fingers so that they form a large "V," moving the pinkie and ring fingers together to the right and the middle and index fingers together to the left.**

3.   **Fully extend the thumb so that it is perpendicular to the hand.**

9. 　　　**THE POUND**

Usage and
Origins:

The fists of two people make contact in a series of choreographed motions. The pound gesture is an urban greeting borne of the streets. It is a much cooler incarnation of the secret handshakes invented by children and enables the user to greet friends without resorting to the handshake gesture, which can be seen as too formal, or the hug gesture, which can be too personal. The pound gesture is both aggressive and familiar, allowing the gesturer to be welcoming without shedding his carefully cultivated cool. It takes some time to perform and is more common in laid-back situations when time is not of the essence.

Region:

This is an urban, American gesture and will not likely be seen much outside the United States. In recent years, the pound gesture has spread to suburban areas where youths congregate and many college campuses across the United States.

Environment:

A bustling metropolitan street corner or any area where hip city kids are saying "hello" or "goodbye" is a good place to see the pound in action. Keep in mind that this is an informal gesture and should not be used in professional or formal settings. It came about on the streets and has yet to stray far from them.

Execution: The pound gesture is a gesture that involves two people.

1. Make a fist with one hand [FIG. A].

2. Approach someone else, usually one you are familiar with but have not seen for some time. This person will also make a fist with one hand.

3. Turn your fist so that your knuckles are facing out and your thumb is on top.

4. Extend your fist into the space between you and the other person at waist level. The other person will do the same.

5. The other person will reach out and gently hit the thumb-end of your fist with the pinkie-end of his of her fist [FIG. B]. After hitting, his or her fist will hover in the air above your fist.

6. Remove your hand from below the other person's fist and bring it up and over his or her fist.

7. Gently hit the thumb-end of his or her fist with the pinkie-end of your own.

8. Pull your fist away from the central space. Some people will turn their fists so that their knuckles face the ground.

9. Move your fist toward the other person while they do the same, and strike the fingers of your fists together once [FIG. C].

10. Separate from the person.

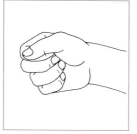

FIG. A

FIG. B

Fig. C

10. **THE SALUTE**

Usage and Origins:

A flat hand is raised palm-down to touch the forehead. In its modern use, the salute gesture is a formal, required gesture of respect that is to be performed by someone of lower military rank toward someone of higher military rank. The officer who is lower ranking salutes the higher-ranking officer, holding the pose until the latter responds in kind, then both drop their hands.

If the proper respect is not shown to an outranking officer, disciplinary action will likely be taken. The salute gesture is one of the few formal gestures of respect that is still in use in Western society—most other such gestures have fallen out of practice with the rise of egalitarian government.

Historians disagree over the origin of the salute gesture. Some propose that it has its origin in medieval times, when a knight would raise his visor to show an approaching knight that he meant no harm. Others postulate that its roots can be found in the formal hat-tip to a superior in more recent centuries (see Tɪᴘ ᴏꜰ ᴛʜᴇ Hᴀᴛ, page 30). The salute gesture has been in use as a sign of respect among military officers for at least several centuries—one historian cites a British rule book from 1745 that called for soldiers to "clap up their hands to their hats and bow" as superiors passed.

Though the exact origin of the salute is still in dispute, it is certain that it is second nature for those in the military and other areas of law enforcement, but it will rarely be seen outside this context. When it is, it is often in jest—civilians may poke fun at a friend by saluting, implying that the person saluted is bossy and controlling.

Region: You will find ranking officers saluting one another in any nation that employs a military defense system. You will not see the salute in tribal societies. Be cognizant of where you point a salute in Italy, where it can also mean "You're crazy."

Environment: Basic-training camps, military bases, and battlefields are all good places to see the salute in action.

Execution: This salute is the formal military version.

    1.   Stand at attention, with arms at your sides, shoulders back, and eyes staring straight ahead.

    2.   Hold your right hand flat, with fingers pressed together [FIG. A].

    3.   Raise your right elbow out and to the side as you bring the fingertips of that hand to your right eyebrow.

    4.   Hold the pose until the subject being saluted has passed, or you are given permission to stop.

    5.   Drop the hand straight down to your side.

FIG. A

Variations of
Performance:

In Germany and Eastern Europe, a salute with two straight fingers (rather than a flat hand) is performed as a sign of white power by neo-Nazis [Fig. B], and recently, a three-fingered salute was used by opponents of Slobodan Milosevic in Belgrade, Yugoslavia.

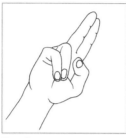

Fig. B

---

11.   **TIP OF THE HAT**

Usage and
Origins:

An imaginary hat is tipped. Tipping an imaginary hat originates from a time when hats were worn by men and tipped as a gesture of greeting, often toward women. Perhaps around the same time that doors stopped being opened for the "fairer sex," men ceased wearing hats as a matter of course, and the phantom hat-tip gesture became popular.

Nowadays, this gesture is most often performed

tongue-in-cheek by men who wish to seem gallant or by women who wish to throw gender stereotypes out the window. In a rare occurrence, one might witness a person tipping the hat in all seriousness, to let another know he or she has been noticed and appreciated.

Rarer still, the hat-tip greeting might be used in homage to a simpler, more chivalrous time.

Region: Western countries such as the United States and Britain, whose fashion cultures once included a stunning array of headwear, will recognize the tip of the hat gesture.

Environment: Though it is now rare to see this gesture employed as a greeting, it will still occur on the odd street corner or in a dimly lit restaurant.

The more ironic use of the gesture can be seen at parties, in meetings, or in a neighborhood watering hole.

Execution:
1. **Place your thumb against your top fingers, so that your hand resembles a duck bill.**

2. **Raise your arm up so that it is at a 90-degree angle, with your hand near your forehead.**

3. Position your hand so that the tips of your
    fingers are almost touching your forehead.

4. Gently nod your head forward, while moving
    your hand slightly upward.

Variations of
Performance:

For the very gallant, a deep, sweeping bow may
accompany this gesture.

12.   **WAVING**

Usage and
Origins:

The hand is raised and moved from side to side. This
common gesture of friendly greeting and farewell has
its origins as a distress symbol, since it is one of the
simplest and most obvious ways to make oneself visi-
ble from a distance. Because it is such a good way to
draw attention, it also grew to be a common greeting,
calling attention to oneself as one approaches.

The waving gesture is used in a variety of situations and locales, and unless it is accompanied by
other signs of distress, you should interpret it to
mean a simple "hello" or "goodbye."

Region:

This gesture is understood worldwide but is less
common in Italy (see "Variations of Performance,"
page 34). The largely American back-and-forth motion
of this gesture is often initially interpreted by

Europeans to mean "no" and thus should be used with caution in Parisian cafés and German brewhouses—especially if you do want more to drink.

Environment: The waving gesture will be seen in situations ranging from airport arrivals to beauty pageant parades. Special occasions like the first day of school will produce frequent waves, sometimes accompanied by deeply felt tears. The waving gesture will also be seen in such mundane settings as the corner grocery store, the post office, or your own driveway.

Execution: 1. **Extend the arm fully above the head or just above shoulder level, palm out.**

2. **Tilt the hand at the wrist from side to side, waving in a small arc, or rotate slightly from sided to side [FIG. A].**

FIG. A

| Variations of Performance: | In Europe, the waving gesture is often accomplished with the thumb straight out, with a flapping motion caused by bending at the wrist. This is commonly seen when adults are waving to children, or when children are waving at each other. |

Another variation is specific to Italy: The hand is waved in the air, but the palm is faced toward the body instead of toward the person to whom you are waving. This variation is derived from patting someone on the back while hugging, and though it looks a lot like that action, it can also be mistaken for the come here gesture (see page 193) by non-Italians.

II. Approval

13. 📷 APPLAUSE

Usage and
Origins:

The hands are repeatedly struck against one another to make a slapping sound. Clapping is perhaps the most effusive of the gestures used to indicate approval. It is generally understood to mean that some act, whether it be a performance, a goal, or a laudatory announcement, is cause for celebration. The happiness conveyed by the smacking noise of palm against palm is perhaps one of the most satisfying sounds there is for a performer of any type.

Region:

Though applause as an appreciative gesture is almost universal, there are a few nuances to its meaning around the world. In parts of Asia, such as China, applause is sometimes used as a greeting, and Russian ballet dancers may applaud their audience.

In Central and Eastern Europe, audiences will clap in rhythm, often to music, as a sign of approval. In North America, this same type of clapping can also be used at concerts to express approval and unity, or it can be a sign of impatience before the show or an encore, letting the performer know the audience is ready to be entertained.

In parts of Southeast Asia, such as Japan, an

audience will applaud until the musicians leave the
stage at the symphony—in the United States,
performers rarely leave until after the audience stops
clapping.

Environment: Clapping comes about from excitement and congratulations, two feelings that make themselves known in
many arenas. Sporting events, dramatic performances,
concerts, and even just a good joke around the dinner
table can be cause for applause.

Execution: 1. **Extend both hands in front of your body.**

2. **Smack one palm against the other palm, making
an audible slapping sound.**

3. **Repeat.**

Variations of
Performance: The standing ovation is a higher level of applause
that shows that a performance moved the audience
members to the point of rising from their seats while
clapping.

14.   **ARMS UP**

Usage and
Origins: *Both arms are extended up in the air.* This fairly simple
gesture has several meanings, and you'll be able to tell

what is meant by the situation you're in. The arms up gesture is most commonly performed at times of celebration, as when a goal is scored or a peak is reached. Throwing one's arms into the air appears to make the body larger or more grand, and the person celebrating the victory will feel taller or more dominant.

Another appropriate time to use this gesture is at a crime scene, but only if you've been caught. Law enforcement officials instruct suspected criminals to come out with their hands up, meaning that they should raise their arms with hands open to show that they're unarmed and not going to fight. In this context, performing the arms up gesture renders you defenseless.

This gesture may also be used to casually admit defeat or wrongdoing; if a spouse or family member accuses you of a minor infraction or beats you in a game of cards, you may raise your arms in admittance of failure or defeat.

Finally, raising the arms into the air is an ancient posture of prayer, with open palms reaching toward the sky, and therefore, toward God or some higher power. In this position, one is thought to be attempting to embrace the Almighty.

Region: When used in celebration or surrender, this gesture is common the world over, since victory and defeat are both universal. For holier purposes, the arms up gesture will be most often seen where prayer is a more public practice, as in predominately Muslim nations.

Environment: As either a sign of celebration or defeat, the arms up gesture will be seen in sports arenas, stadiums, and parks. Both sides, at one time or another, may feel the urge to throw their arms in the air, except in the case of a tie, when neither team will feel particularly elated or depressed.

Final exam periods are good times to witness college students reveling in good scores or simply in the fact that exams have been completed. Any time good news is given—such as in the delivery room of a hospital, your living room after the winning lottery numbers are announced, or the office when you've received word of a promotion—will be the place to see this gesture put to good use.

The "I surrender" posture will be seen outside of a bank when a robbery has been thwarted, or outside of a convenience store once hostages have been safely released.

When used in prayer, the arms up gesture will be seen at mosques, churches, temples, or any place where the spirit moves people.

Execution: 1. **Raise both arms straight up into the air.**

2. **Lock your elbows to keep your arms straight.**

For a more relaxed version, the arms can remain slightly bent.

3. The hands can be held rigid and flat, in fists, or somewhere in between.

4. Hold the pose briefly.

5. Drop your arms to your sides.

Variations of Performance: The hands may be clasped above the head once they are in the air, often to celebrate a win in a sporting event, such as a boxing match.

---

15. **THE BUTT PAT**

Usage and Origins: *The posterior of one person is gently patted by another person's hand.* The butt pat gesture originated in American football. Experts speculate that the original intent was a traditional pat on the shoulder to signify that a good play was carried out. However, since the shoulder pads used in football are necessarily massive, pats to the shoulder went unnoticed by the player. The most viable alternative to the shoulder must have been the posterior, and this gesture has been a congratulatory one ever since.

You will rarely see the butt pat gesture employed

by a woman, nor are you likely to see it used in polite company off the playing field. Due to the seemingly intimate nature of this gesture and the fact that it comes about during the intensely passionate course of a competitive game, it is imperative to use this gesture only in the accepted realm—that is, the sporting arena.

Region: North Americans and Europeans use this gesture quite often, but you'll be hard-pressed to find it elsewhere. The rest of the world seems to fall back on more commonplace gestures of celebration when a teammate makes a tough play, such as a hug.

Environment: As previously mentioned, this is a gesture that is only to be used during a sporting event, on the playing field, whether the field is Shea Stadium or your backyard. Users could be professionals in full-gear or friends in jeans and T-shirts.

Execution: The butt pat is a gesture that involves two people.

1. **Approach another person, usually a teammate, from behind [FIG. A].**

2. **Place one hand loosely at your side, palm forward, fingers together.**

3. Quickly slap the bottom of the other person's butt, usually toward the outer edge [Fig. B].

4. Offer a verbal compliment regarding the player's skill on the field.

Fig. A   Fig. B

 THE HIGH FIVE

Usage and Origins:

The palms of two people are slapped together high in the air. This celebratory gesture is one that originated in American team sports; when one player made a good shot, blocked the other team's goal, or ran several yards in one play, another player congratulated him with a high five—the five fingers of each player's hands slapped above their heads. From the sports arena, the high five crossed over and gained popularity as a gesture of greeting in the last decades of the twentieth century.

These days, the high five has gone the way of acid-washed jeans and paint-splatter prints; it is no longer considered a hip move. It could even be said that this gesture is now reserved mainly for squares who are trying to seem cool—yuppies who are trying to hang onto their once-prized hipness. When one such person wishes to perform the gesture, he will raise one arm expectantly. Even if no one reciprocates, it will be clear what gesture was intended.

Region:
The high five gesture will generally be seen in the United States, and with the permeation of American culture abroad, there is a chance to witness this gesture around the globe.

Environment:
Since this gesture is still used to celebrate a sporting victory, it will be seen most often in stadiums, on basketball courts, and on playing fields.

The tongue-in-cheek high five will be seen in bars during trivia competitions or in restaurants and clubs when friends effusively celebrate another's pick-up style.

Execution:
The high five is a gesture that involves two people.

1. Approach your partner with one arm extended vertically into the air. The arm can be slanted slightly; it does not have to be parallel to your body.

2. Keep your palm open, facing the oncoming person.

3. Your partner should mimic your motion.

4. Make hand-to-hand contact with your partner's hand, emphatically hitting the open palm with your own. A smacking sound will be audible.

5. Retreat.

Variations of Performance:

Sometimes you will be exhorted to "Gimme five down low" after a high five, or even just on its own. This involves slapping another's palm at about waist level.

Similarly, you may be asked to "Slip me some skin"; here, it is expected that you will not smack but will instead rub the other person's palm with your own.

Finally, any of these, including the high five itself, may be accomplished using both hands; this is sometimes referred to as "giving 10."

17. 📷   **NOD "YES"**

Usage and Origins:

The head is moved up and down repeatedly. As is apparent from its name, this is the definitive gesture of approval. Experts believe that the nod of assent is derived from the downward motion of an infant's head as it takes its mother's breast for nursing, though it may also be a shortened version of the submissive bow (see page 4), in which case the message may also be "Yes, you're right."

The uses for this gesture are virtually endless; any time a question requires an affirmative answer is a time to use the nod "yes" gesture. The gesture is so common that the nod "yes" gesture is often simply called "nodding," despite the fact that nodding no is also feasible (see Nod "No," page 69.)

Region:

In most of the world, you'll find that this gesture is used to mean "yes," with a few important exceptions. In parts of Greece, Bulgaria, the former Yugoslavia, Turkey, and Iran, this gesture means the exact opposite. That is, the up-and-down nod actually means "no," while the right-to-left version—which means "no" everywhere else—means "yes" (see page 69).

Environment:

Except for the countries noted above, you would be hard-pressed to find a venue where the nod isn't used and seen—it is almost universally understood.

Execution: 1. Tilt your head straight back, raising your chin in the air.

2. Drop your head straight down, lowering your chin toward your body.

3. Repeat several times.

Note: The distance you move your head will depend on the situation and your personal style.

18. **OKAY**

Usage and Origins: *An "O" is made with the thumb and index finger with the rest of the fingers extended.* This gesture is most commonly used to express the colloquial term "okay," as a signal of approval or agreement. Experts disagree over when "okay" made its first appearance in our language. Some say that the term was first used on March 23, 1839, in an article in the *Boston Morning Post*, when a writer deliberately misspelled "all correct" as "oll korrect" (deliberately misspelling words was a short-lived fad, popular at that time). This was then shortened to "OK." Verbal usage eventually led to the term being generally spelled out as "okay."

Others say the term came from the 1840s, as an abbreviation for presidential candidate Martin Van

Buren's nickname, "Old Kinderhook." Still other experts think "OK" is meant as the opposite of the boxing term "K.O." ("knockout"). Regardless of the precise origin, the colloquial expression became quite popular in the nineteenth century, and it was even used in a popular song in the 1860s in England.

Though there is also confusion over whether the gesture or the expression came first, these days it is the single best-known gesture in the United States, with 98 percent recognition. The gesture's use as a sign of approval may have had its origin in universal, unconscious conversational movement, when the tip of the thumb and the tip of the index finger are brought together to emphasize a precise point.

Early references to the thumb–index finger ring as a gesture of approval appear in the writings of the Roman Quintillian during the first century A.D., as well as in seventeenth-century English writings. These days it is generally believed that in the formation of the gesture the index finger and thumb form the "O," while the other three fingers form the "K."

Less popularly, this gesture can suggest an orifice—the anus or vagina—and this meaning can be seen on early Greek vase paintings. If the thumb–index finger ring is used in this context, it is an insult ("You are an orifice" or "You are a homosexual") but might also be beseeching ("I'd like to have sex with you"). In this manner, the gesture was used on amulets, originally to ward off the evil eye. It is still a good-luck charm in Greece.

Still another use for this gesture is to imply that one is worthless or no good, with the thumb–index finger ring meaning zero instead of the letter "O." This meaning is not as common as "okay," but it is practiced in many of the same areas as the dominant "okay" connotation, leading to potential confusion over which meaning is implied.

Finally, this gesture can mean "change," but only in Japan. The shape of the fingers resembles a coin, and one may non-verbally ask for change in coins with this gesture.

Region: The okay gesture is called "American OK" by non-English speakers, due to the varied meanings of the gesture in other parts of the world. As a gesture of acceptance, the okay gesture is most popular in North America, in most of Europe, and where the influence of Western culture is felt around the globe.

The gesture is recognized for its other meanings in various parts of the world. It will be taken to mean "orifice" in Germany, Tunisia, Greece, Turkey, Russia, the Middle East, and parts of South America.

The "worthless" meaning will shine through in Belgium, France, and Tunisia.

As noted above, in Japan, it stands for "change."

Environment: Because of its multifarious meanings, this gesture will be seen in a variety of places. From high school hallways to urban street corners to outdoor markets, you are likely to see this gesture most anywhere.

Execution: 1. **Make a circle with the thumb and index finger.**

2. **Splay out your remaining fingers.**

3. **Pump once.**

4. **Release.**

Variations of Performance: Push the index finger of your other hand through the ring repeatedly for a crude gesture that stands for sex (see SEX FINGERS, page 126). In Italy, when the ring points down, the okay gesture can mean justice, as if one is holding the scales of justice between the thumb and index finger.

19.   **RAISE THE ROOF**

Usage and Origins: *The hands, facing upward near the ears, are raised and lowered repeatedly.* Though various American college sports teams claim that they created this gesture, experts actually give football star Emmit Smith the credit for its invention. Like many gestures that originated in the sporting world, this one has gone from the playing field to the street and beyond in recent years. The implication of the raise the roof gesture is that whatever has just happened is so incredible or wonderful that the roof of the building must be elevated to contain the resulting excitement.

You'll often see this gesture in a large crowd of people, such as a college party, where excitement mounts as alcohol flows.

Region: You'll find this gesture almost solely in the United States, though due to the spreading influence of American culture, you may notice the rare occurrence in Europe or Asia.

Environment: Sports arenas and stadiums are popular places to see the raise the roof gesture in use, as are fraternity houses and bars in college towns.

Execution: 1. **Raise both arms straight above your head.**

2. **Orient your hands so they are horizontal, palms open to the sky.**

3. **Pump your forearms, raising your hands from your shoulders to the top of your head each time.** [Fig. A].

4. Repeat at least twice but no more than four times.

5. Sometimes an enthusiastic shout of "Raise the roof!" makes a nice complement to the gesture.

6. Lower your arms.

FIG. A

20. **SMILE**

Usage and
Origins:

The corners of the mouth are lifted. Known to some experts as the "ultimate gesture," smiling evolved from pulling the lips back from the teeth as a sign of fear. From there, though, it became a signal of peace and then friendship. The smile is a gesture that is unique to the human species and one that can be observed as early as infancy.

You are likely to see the smile used throughout your day as a sign of acknowledgment, happiness, or loving feelings on the part of the gesturer. The appropriate response to the smile is to flash one in return.

When a photographer says, "Say cheese!" the proper thing to do is smile.

Region: A smile will be seen as a friendly gesture the world over, with a few caveats. In parts of Southeast Asia, such as Singapore, Malaysia, and the Philippines, a person will often attempt to mask embarrassment by smiling or laughing.

In Japan it is not customary to smile for government photographs such as licenses or passports.

In Korea, excessive smiling is taken to mean that an individual is shallow or thoughtless, so use this gesture in moderation.

Environment: Locations where pleasant feelings need to be conveyed are places to see a smile. You'll experience a smile at the grocery store, on the bus, or in the office. Merriment is something that often occurs spontaneously and therefore will produce smiles at any time and in any place.

Execution: 1. Turn the corners of the lips up.

2. Simultaneously spread the lips until the teeth show. Generally, the teeth are held loosely together, and just the lips—not the whole mouth—are opened.

3. If you possess them, dimples will appear.

Variations of Performance:

Often, a smile may be phony; the gesturer may want to convey feelings of happiness or acceptance but not actually feel them. You can tell a fake smile by looking at the corners of the smiler's eyes—if they aren't wrinkled, he or she probably doesn't mean it.

---

21. **THUMBS-UP**

Usage and Origins:

The thumb is extended from a closed fist. This ubiquitous gesture of approval was long thought to come from ancient Rome, when the Colosseum hosted gladiator fights on a regular basis. It was thought to occur thusly: The emperor would ask the crowd if a gladiator ought to be set free or whether he should be killed. If the crowd pointed its thumbs up, it meant that the gladiator ought to be let go; thumbs pointed down meant that he should be slain.

Recently, however, experts have come to believe

that this popular knowledge is false, based on bad Latin translations. New research suggests that the Romans actually hid their thumbs to spare the gladiator, displaying a closed fist, and showed their thumbs to have him slain, producing a thumb-out.

In light of these recent discoveries, experts continue to research the exact origin of the positive thumbs-up gesture. One possibility comes from the Old English saying, "Here's my thumb on it," which was used to seal a bargain. Two people moistened their thumbs and then made contact with each other's thumb. Another origin for the positive meaning may come from the French, who indicate the number one with a thumb.

Though the origin of the thumbs-up gesture is still somewhat unknown, the meanings and occurrences are various. It will most often be used to signify agreement or assent to a question that is asked. Where would Arthur Fonzarelli from *Happy Days* be without the thumbs-up gesture? And in most parts of the world, hitchhikers who are desperate for a ride would be hard-pressed to find a better way of letting motorists know their intentions, as the extended thumb is the nearly universal way to hitch a ride (see "Region," below, for some exceptions).

Region: As a gesture of approval, the thumbs-up gesture is widespread, practiced in North America and most of

Europe. The thumbs-up gesture is also seen in other parts of the world as an imported Western gesture.

However, it is important to be aware of some alternate meanings. In Japan, extending the thumb refers to a male companion—any male, whether it be husband, friend, boss, or son. (Extending the pinkie represents a female companion.) The thumb can also mean the number five in Japan.

Be cautious using this gesture in Northwest Spain, where it is a political signal flashed in support of the Basque separatist movement. In Nigeria and Australia, the thumbs-up gesture is an unmitigated indication of insult, especially when jerked upward, so use it sparingly, if at all, in these areas.

Environment: Due to the varying nature of the meanings of this gesture, you're likely to encounter it throughout your daily life in any number of locales. Anywhere one might like to agree or encourage another, such as in restaurants, offices, hospitals, or playing fields, is a place to see the thumbs-up gesture in use.

Execution: 1. Make a fist with one hand.

2. Extend your thumb perpendicular to the fist.

3. Turn your fist so that the thumb is sticking straight into the air.

4. Crook your elbow and extend your hand approximately waist-high, or extend the arm to its full length directly in front of you.

Variations of Performance:

Though not as popular and having an entirely opposite meaning, the thumbs-down gesture has achieved some notoriety in recent years due to the movie rating system of Roger Ebert and the late Gene Siskel. This gesture is performed in the same manner as the thumbs-up gesture, but has the thumb pointing, predictably, downward. It is used in situations where disapproval needs to be conveyed.

22. **THE WAVE**

Usage and Origins:

A group of people simulate the ocean's swell by standing and raising both arms, then sitting and lowering them. In the world of gestures, there is perhaps none more communal than the wave. It is a true display of support and celebration, and it shows how serious fans can be about their favorite teams. It is interesting that such a unifying gesture would have such disputed origins.

The Huskies, the University of Washington's football team, claim to have invented it. They purport that Rob Weller, a former Huskies cheerleader, and Bill Bissel, the bandleader, completed the first wave on October 31, 1981.

Some sports and gesture experts, however, support a second theory, that Krazy George, a 32-year sports-entertainment veteran, invented the wave 16 days prior to the Huskies game, on October 15, 1981, at a nationally televised Major League baseball playoff game in Oakland, California.

Even now, more than two decades and countless waves later, this is a hotly debated topic, with Internet chat rooms and message boards inflamed over who should get the credit for creating the wave.

Despite the controversy, the wave is a way for fans to rally in support of their team, generating excitement in both the players and the spectators. However, it is generally agreed that after three rounds of waving, fans should rest a bit.

Region: Though the wave began as an American fanatical gesture, exuberant sports fans exist the world over. It didn't take long for the wave to make its way to sporting events in Italy, Argentina, and beyond.

Environment: You'll see this gesture on display in stadiums and arenas, on courts and fields, and even in your living room during a particularly enthusiastic evening of Monday night football, provided you have several people in your living room.

Execution: The wave requires a group of people, usually a stadium mostly full of fans. Generally, one enthusiastic fan will get the wave started by enticing one group to begin, and the fever spreads willingly. As an individual participating in the wave, prepare as follows:

1. As the wave approaches, clear the space around the seat of any accumulated debris, and empty the lap of food, programs, children, or jackets.

2. When the person next to you stands, begin to rise from your seat [FIG. A].

3. Simultaneously raise you arms from straight at your sides to straight into the air as the person next to you lowers his or her arms.

4. Time it so that your arms reach their apex just as your body becomes fully upright [FIG. B].

5. Lower your arms and sit back down.

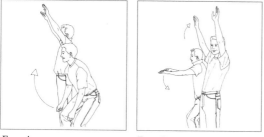

Fig. A   Fig. B

Variations of   The wave may be accompanied by a loud cheer as the
Performance: performers stand up, making the wave gesture an
                 auditory as well as visual celebration.

III. Disapproval

23. **ARMS AKIMBO**

Usage and Origins:

The hands are placed on the hips. Though this gesture is sometimes simply an unconscious use of body language, it will often be a deliberate sign that something is not quite right.

The word "akimbo" comes from Old Norse, and means "bent like a bow," which suggests an archer's bow that is ready to fire an arrow. Hence this gesture, which is often called "hands on hips," has come to be understood as a defensive pose that experts label an "anti-embrace." Its implications are clearly antisocial, and it will often be seen in situations where a group wants to exclude an individual.

Sports players will be seen in this posture after losing a game, and those in an argument are likely to take this stance when an impasse is reached. The stern expression on the face of the gesturer will let you know how serious the issue is.

Region:

The arms akimbo gesture will be seen worldwide, but in areas of Southeast Asia such as Malaysia and the Philippines, it is more seriously enacted and received, as it signifies extreme, seething rage.

Environment: Since it is virtually imperative that the gesturer be
                standing in order to enact this pose, areas where foes
                meet while upright will see this gesture the most.
                Sporting arenas will be a common venue for this ges-
                ture, as will middle-school recess areas, and perhaps
                even courtrooms and police stations.

Execution: 1. **Spread your legs to shoulder width.**

                2. **Place your hands on your hips, elbows out.**

Variations of   The single arm held akimbo, with one hand on one
Performance: hip, carries a similar connotation, but may be con-
                strued as less serious and slightly more cocky.

24.   **ARMS FOLDED**

Usage and   *The arms are folded across the chest.* When a person
Origins: folds his arms across his chest in a deliberate gesture,
                you know he means business. Though this defensive
                gesture is often simply an unconscious bit of body
                language, it can also be a measured tactic used to
                intimidate or exclude another person. Prison and
                security guards use this gesture as an indication of
                slight threat, or as a reminder that another is not
                allowed to pass.

                    Folding your arms across your chest can also be

an indicator of the need to put a barrier between yourself and an uncomfortable social situation.

Region: Uncomfortable situations, disagreements, and guards are prevalent the world over; this gesture is not limited to one region of the globe.

Environment: Anywhere that a fight may break out—from parking lots to public parks—is a place to see this gesture in use. Similarly, anywhere that guards are needed— prisons, lobbies of skyscrapers, and even department stores—will see arms folded over chests. Bouncers, who are guards of a sort, often adopt this pose while manning the doors of bars and clubs in order to intimidate and assert authority.

Execution: 1. **Bend your arms at the elbows.**

    2. **Fold your arms so that they cross your body.**

    3. **Intertwine your arms as is most comfortable.**

    4. **Spread your legs to shoulder width.**

    Note: Experts have discovered that there are actually six different ways to fold the arms, with varying positions for the hands in each. The assorted postures have no different meaning, and

the use of them seems to depend on personal preference and comfort.

25.   **THE CHOKE**

Usage and Origins:

The hands are wrapped around the gesturer's or another's throat. The choke is versatile in that it may be performed on one's own person or on another, and contact is not necessary in order to do it. Sometimes merely performing the gesture in the air accomplishes the same goal. Another aspect of the versatility of the choke gesture is in its varied meanings across cultures.

It may come from the reflexive movement of grabbing your throat when something is lodged in it (hence, the Red Cross's suggestion that this gesture ought to be used in order to let others know there is an emergency). This, however, is hardly the most common or accepted use of the choke gesture, and regionality will certainly dictate meaning.

Region:

Often thought of as simply a frustrated gesture, signaling the desire to choke another to death, this gesture's meanings are actually multifarious. In North America, the Red Cross suggests that it be used as the official choke signal, as in, "I'm choking. Who here knows the Heimlich maneuver?"

Also in North America, as well as parts of the

Middle East, the common meaning that you are so fed up that you would like to choke another applies.

A less common use of the gesture in North America is when a person wants to convey that he or she "choked," or didn't perform well due to stress or pressure.

In Italy, it is a way to express being fed up, or "I've had it up to here."

In areas of South America, the choke signifies imprisonment. In this case, the gesture may be used to show that someone is in prison or may go to prison, or that a particular behavior could land one in jail (which is why the term "the choke" is sometimes used as slang for "jail").

Finally, in New Guinea, the choke is used to show that the gesturer or another person wants to commit suicide or that someone actually has.

Environment: For the Red Cross–accepted meaning of the gesture, a restaurant, bar, the dinner table, or any other place where food ingestion occurs will see this gesture used frantically.

Otherwise, since frustration and nervousness are easy to come by, the choke will be seen in any number of locales, from sports venues to stage shows.

Execution: 1. **Raise both hands to your throat.**

2. **Cup your throat between the thumb and fingers of each hand, overlapping your hands but not intertwining them.**

3. **Shake your hands against the throat.**

4. **Bulge your eyes to convey urgency.**

Variations of   If both hands are unavailable, this gesture may be per-
Performance: formed using only one hand. Additionally, you can
               reach out to another person's neck and simulate the
               act of choking her, if she is the source of frustration.

26.   **EYEBROW FURROW**

Usage and   *The eyebrows are angled sternly.* This gesture, which
Origins: shows acute emotion, is often regarded as an uncon-
             scious bit of body language. However, it can also be
             used deliberately as a response to pain, grief, or dis-
             pleasure.

             Also called the "knit" eyebrow, you'll express ele-
             ments of fear and anger by invoking this gesture. This
             expression will also be used to express deep concen-
             tration on a puzzling or intense subject and may be a
             sign of curiosity or confusion.

The eyebrow furrow is a gesture that may be used as a "helping" gesture as well; it adds weight to another gesture, such as ARMS FOLDED (see page 60) or ARMS AKIMBO (see page 59).

Region: Confusion, curiosity, and anxiety are unfortunately prevalent across cultures, so you'll see this gesture all over the world, with no significant difference in meaning.

Environment: Teachers from elementary to high school will use the eyebrow furrow gesture to express seriousness or displeasure with their students.

Anywhere that deep concentration is required—from the library to the theater to the interrogation room—will see eyebrows furrowed.

Execution: 1. **Lower your brows and bring them together, taking care not to cross your eyes.**

2. **Scrunch your nose.**

3. **Stare—either at a specific object or into the distance.**

27. 📷   **FINGER WAG**

Usage and
Origins:

The index finger is shaken back and forth. The finger wag carries with it a mild reprimand and has a negative, though non-threatening, connotation. The message is "No, don't do that" or "That's naughty" and is used to admonish but not to intimidate. It is, however, a gesture that is used to dominate and make the person on the receiving end feel smaller; the finger is like a mini-club that is being shaken in order to shame another. Parents are proponents of this gesture, often using it in disciplinary situations.

This gesture has become so much a part of the canon that the term "finger-wagging" has become a metaphor for any type of cautionary attitude or rule-making.

Region: Since parents scold children the world over, the finger wag will be seen worldwide. In Japan, however, the same meaning is implied when one waggles the whole hand with the palm out.

Environment: Teachers and parents are the biggest performers of this gesture, so school yards, classrooms, and mini-vans are the most common spots to see it in use. Anywhere a little cautionary discipline is necessary will be a place to see the finger wag firsthand.

Execution: 1. Make a fist [FIG. A].

2. Extend your index finger [FIG. B].

3. Raise your arm so that your hand is at face level, to one side.

4. Tilt the index finger from side to side laterally, keeping the finger straight and in the same plane as the back of your hand.

5. If you want, shake your head in harmony with the tilting of your finger, to emphasize the "no" you are trying to convey.

FIG. A

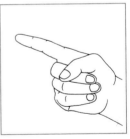

FIG. B

28. 📷   **LOSER**

Usage and
Origins:

An "L" is formed with the index finger and thumb and displayed on the forehead. A fairly new invention, the loser gesture dates back to 1994, when Jim Carrey's movie *Ace Ventura: Pet Detective* took theaters by storm. Carrey's character used the "L" on the forehead as his trademark gesture, making sure everyone who didn't measure up knew it.

The startling popularity and success of the film made the gesture commonplace for a brief span in the mid-1990s, spawning sightings in other hit films such as *Clueless* and *Jerry Maguire*. These days, the gesture is generally confined to use by children and adolescents, and then only to good-naturedly make fun of friends.

Region:

The loser gesture will rarely, if ever, be seen outside North America, where film taglines and trademark gestures are most often imitated ad nauseum.

Environment:

In the mid-1990s, it was fairly common to see this gesture performed outside of movie theaters across the United States, but these days, the loser gesture will generally be confined to school recess areas, malls, and other locations where teens and pre-teens are given free reign to make fun of their contemporaries.

Execution: Though you may think that it matters which hand you use when performing this gesture, it is done with either the left or the right hand with little regard to whether the "L" is legible to the loser or not.

1. Make a fist with one hand.

2. Extend your index finger.

3. Extend your thumb to form an "L."

4. Raise your hand and place the "L" against your forehead.

5. Say "Loser" with derision, generally elongating the first syllable.

---

29.   **NOD "NO"**

Usage and Origins: *The head is shaken from side to side.* Perhaps the most common gesture of disapproval in existence, the nod "no" is often simply referred to as "shaking one's head." It is used in all types of situations where a "no" is required, and often adds emphasis to a verbal refusal when one is able to be given. When words are unavailable, such as in the dentist's chair or when you are eating, there will be little mistaking what you mean when you perform the nod "no" gesture.

This gesture originates in infancy—a baby will shake his head emphatically back and forth to indicate refusal of food at his mother's breast or when he is being spoon-fed and disapproves or no longer wishes to eat.

Region: Displeasure and discontentment know no culture, but there are some parts of the globe in which the usual nod "no" gesture will indicate the opposite of what you may intend. In Bulgaria, parts of Greece, Turkey, Iran, and the former Yugoslavia, if you shake your head back and forth, it will be taken as a "yes," while up and down means "no."

Further, in Greece, Italy, Malta, and Tunisia, an abrupt toss of your head backward, coupled with jerking your chin up and raising your eyebrows, means "no."

Finally, in Saudi Arabia and other parts of the Middle East, people jerk their heads back and click their tongues to indicate disapproval.

Environment: It is necessary to indicate disapproval in virtually all areas of life, from the grocery store to the conference room to the dinner table. It would be difficult to find a location that hasn't seen the nod "no" gesture.

Execution:	1. **Twist your head to one side, pointing toward one shoulder.**
	2. **Twist your head around toward the other shoulder.**
	3. **Repeat several times.**

Note: The distance you swivel your head will depend on the situation and your personal style.

Variations of Performance:	In Ethiopia, a local variation for the nod "no" is performed by turning your head sharply to one side and then back to the center.

30. **NOSE HOLD**

Usage and Origins:	*The nostrils are closed with the thumb and index finger.* There is nothing mysterious or anecdotal about the birth of this gesture: When something has an unpleasant odor, instinct tells you to block it, and the best way to do this is to shut off your sense of smell.

While attempting to keep a bad smell from assailing your senses is more of a reflex than a gesture, the act of holding your nose becomes a gesture when it is done to warn others of a noxious odor they may be approaching.

When a person leaves a kitchen in which something has burned, he may hold his nose in order to alert another not to enter the room.

A disgusting public lavatory experience has been known to elicit the "nose hold" warning as well. A performance or person that is thought to metaphorically "stink" may also prompt use of the nose hold gesture.

Region: Sadly, not all aromas are pleasant, so this gesture is fairly universal and widely understood. From big city dumpsters to back country horse farms, people need a warning so as not to be taken by surprise by foul odors.

Environment: Corridors leading to public restrooms are a common place to see this gesture put to good use, as are the entrances to kitchens where things may not have gone according to plan. Of course, bad smells will unfortunately not be limited to these rooms; watch for the nose hold around gym locker rooms, sporting areas in general, and in shoe stores, when customers are embarrassed by stinky feet.

It should be mentioned that sometimes a conventionally good smell will evoke the nose hold; this is likely to happen at perfume counters in department stores, where there is too much of a good thing.

Execution: 1. **Raise one hand to your face.**

2. **Grasp your nose with thumb and forefinger. Leave your other fingers pulled toward your palm.**

3. **Scrunch your nose up slightly.**

4. **Wrinkle your brow.**

Variations of Performance: In Great Britain, this gesture is sometimes accompanied by the free hand pulling an imaginary lavatory chain.

In other cases, you'll see the free hand attempting to wave away the offending odor.

31. 📷 **NOSE WRINKLE**

Usage and Origins: *The nose is scrunched up.* This gesture is so simple as to be almost unconscious at times. You might use it as a reflex when you catch a whiff of a particularly bad smell or when a person you don't care for unexpectedly appears.

When used deliberately, wrinkling the nose expresses dislike or disgust for a person, a situation, or even a food that doesn't suit or please you.

Region: Since wrinkling the nose originated from a reflexive
           bit of body language, its use will be seen worldwide.

Environment: The picnic table or outdoor barbecue area is a com-
                mon place to see this gesture used deliberately, as
                food may sit out and spoil unbeknownst to picnick-
                ers. Outside of cheese shops, near dumpsters in alleys,
                the vicinities of bathrooms, and near lockers at the
                gym are all places where you'll see the nose wrinkle in
                action. Parties and bars where large groups congregate
                might see an increased use of this gesture, as often
                unwanted attendees will cause displeasure.

Execution: 1. **Scrunch your nose up.**

              2. **Squint, if desired.**

32. 📷   **RASPBERRY**

Usage and   *A noise is made with the mouth and tongue that sounds*
Origins: *like flatulence.* Indeed, the raspberry gesture is meant
             to sound like the noises a person with gastrointestinal
             difficulties might make and is therefore a favorite of
             children and vulgar folks everywhere.
                 According to the *Oxford English Dictionary*, the
             name raspberry is taken from "raspberry tart," which
             is Cockney rhyming slang for "fart." Loosely translated

to mean "yuck" or "ugh," the raspberry gesture evolved from the basic gesture of sticking out the tongue in order to reject nourishment from our mother's breast in infancy.

Called the "razzoo" in Australia, the raspberry gesture is often referred to as the "Bronx cheer" in the United States. According to one historian, the name originated in a vaudeville house in the Hub section of the Bronx. A performer there was not up to snuff, and the audience let him know it. The next day, newspapers reported that he received a "Bronx cheer."

Region: The raspberry gesture is used to express displeasure the world over.

Environment: An auditorium or stadium full of particularly crass onlookers might be a good place to see the raspberry gesture in action. Certainly an elementary or middle-school playground, cafeteria, or classroom will be rife with children Bronx-cheering for all they're worth, whether they are unhappy with someone or not.

Execution: 1. **Place your tongue between your top and bottom lips.**

2. **Exhale so that a loud but airy noise is created by the vibration of the tongue.**

Variations of
Performance:

The raspberry gesture can be performed on the skin
of another person, especially a young child, to create
a tickling sensation. In this case it is not meant to
express displeasure—it is more of a funny game.
Favorite places to perform this gesture include bellies
and cheeks.

---

33.   **ROLL OF THE EYES**

Usage and
Origins:

*The eyes traverse a path up, to one side, and back down
again.* Rolling one's eyes can be an unconscious gesture that expresses incredulity, amazement, annoyance,
or frustration. When used intentionally, it will signal
the same emotions.

A favorite of adolescents the world over, the roll of
the eyes generally signifies that a child is fed up with a
parent's harsh rules, assumption of intelligence, or
general inability to be hip. It goes without saying that
the roll of the eyes will *not* be a favorite of parents.

Region:

Since rolling the eyes originated from reflexive body
language, the gesture's use will span most countries of
the world.

Environment:

Anywhere a person wishes to express annoyance or
disbelief will see this gesture in use. The eye roll gesture will be used covertly in a bar or a club between

girlfriends who wish to alert one another that a particularly pathetic pick-up line was used and overtly in the TV room when a child is told to go to bed before she is ready. Any time a story is recounted about an unreliable or outrageous person, the eye roll gesture may be invoked.

Execution:

1. **Starting from a normal position, begin to circle your eyes in their sockets.**

2. **Glance downward to one side, then up along that side, across the top, and back down again.**

3. **Return to a normal position and focus.**

Variations of Performance:

Sometimes, an exaggerated sigh will accompany the roll of the eyes gesture.

34.   **SHAME FINGERS**

Usage and Origins:

One index finger is rubbed across the other. The shame fingers gesture is a deliberate one that lets another—usually a child—know that you are reprimanding her. Experts posit that the rubbing of the fingers symbolizes the friction between the shamer and the shamed. Often, the phrase "Shame on you" will accompany the performance of the gesture.

There is a certain amount of condescension inherent in shaming someone with this gesture; therefore, it is recommended that it not be used with anyone other than small children. The shame fingers may also be used in jest, to sarcastically reprimand another.

Region: The shame fingers gesture will rarely be seen outside of North America, where it has its roots as a gentle rebuke for bad behavior.

Environment: A child's messy bedroom or playroom is the number one spot to see this gesture enacted, as it sends a mild though stern message that a child has been somewhat naughty. For worse behavior, other forms of punishment are often used, rendering the shame fingers gesture a gentler reprimand.

Execution: 1. **Start with both hands held out in front of your chest.**

2. **Make a fist with both hands** [FIG. A].

3. **Extend the index fingers of each hand** [FIG. B].

4. **Brush one index finger over the other, starting at the base of the finger and continuing up to the tip** [FIG. C].

5. Repeat this motion a few times quickly, always returning to the base of the finger to begin.

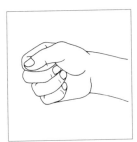

Fig. A

Fig. B

Fig. C

Variations of Performance: A very similar gesture can be found in Wales, Germany, and Austria, wherein the forefingers are moved against each other in a sawing motion. Here it takes the form of an insulting gesture.

35. 📷   **THE SPIT**

Usage and
Origins:

Saliva is expectorated, or the gesturer pretends to spit.
These days, spitting—whether done in general or at a
particular individual—is considered rude, crude, and
insulting across most cultures. Historically, however, a
different set of rules applied.

In the first century A.D., Pliny wrote that spitting
would help to avert witchcraft. The act of spitting is
also mentioned in the New Testament of the Bible;
saliva was put in the eyes of a blind man in order to
restore his sight.

In parts of the Far East such as China, spitting is
considered an act of hygiene and is very acceptable in
public, which is illustrated by the common placement
of spittoons in that part of the world.

Saloons in the United States often have a spittoon,
though whether this is to set a nostalgic mood or for
actual use is up for debate.

Regardless of its overall acceptability, spitting as a
gesture connotes a deep disapproval, as in "I spit on
that, it is unworthy."

Region:

As a gesture to indicate displeasure or disgust, as well
as a bodily function, spitting occurs all over the
world.

Environment: Any locale where a person is disgusted or disappointed by something—whether service, food, or another individual—might be a spot to see someone express their displeasure by spitting, though hopefully it will be only mimed while indoors. Saloons and rodeos will see their fair share of spitting, whether it occurs in spittoons or elsewhere.

Execution: 1. Inhale.

2. Clear the throat.

3. Collect the saliva in the back of the mouth, by the molars. If possible, add mucous to the deposit for increased weight and cohesion.

4. Roll the ball of spit forward on the tongue while pursing the lips.

5. Tuck the chin in against the throat.

6. Aim.

7. Expectorate.

36. 📷 **THROAT SLASH**

Usage and
Origins:

A finger is brought across the throat. Perhaps the utmost gesture of disapproval, the throat slash shows extreme anger, annoyance, and displeasure, whether it is directed at oneself or at another.

When aimed at oneself, this gesture implies embarrassment or rage for doing something silly or stupid in a social situation, thus admitting to the faux pas. It may be more common to see this gesture mimed at another to say, "Cut it out, or else!" The gesturer doesn't actually mean to kill the individual with whom he is annoyed, but the directive to stop the obnoxious behavior should still be heeded.

In very rare instances, some people may actually perform this gesture in order to indicate that another individual—probably one who is not present—is actually slated to be murdered; this seems to occur mainly in popular films.

Region:

This gesture will be enacted to show embarrassment and annoyance around the world.

Environment:

People embarrass themselves all over the place—from parking lots to coffee shops. This gesture will be used to mean "I was so mortified I could have died" in any number of places; likewise for when another person is being obnoxious or unpleasant. The rare meaning that indicates actual murderous feelings will generally be confined to gangster cinema.

Execution:
1. **Make a fist with one hand** [FIG. A].

2. **Extend your index finger** [FIG. B].

3. **Trace a line across your throat with your finger, from ear to ear** [FIG. C].

FIG. A

FIG. B

FIG. C

Variations of
Performance:

In a variation of the throat slash, move a flat palm
across your neck in a cutting motion. This gesture,
which basically translates to "Cut!," originated
behind the scenes in television studios when the on-
air personality needed to finish his act immediately
due to time constraints. These days, it is much more
generally used in the West to mean cut it out, stop
talking, or stop doing whatever it is you are doing.

37.   ◉   **WHATEVER**

Usage and
Origins:

*A "W" is formed with the index finger and thumb of
both hands and displayed in the air.* Made popular by
the 1995 box-office hit *Clueless* starring Alicia
Silverstone, the whatever gesture began as just a word
that was spoken to indicate boredom or displeasure
with a situation or individual. The film appears to be
the first instance that the gesture was paired with the
word, thus creating a trademark made popular by
teens and preteens throughout the mid- to late-1990s.

  This gesture was used by young people to indicate
apathy toward a parent or teacher, irritation at having
to do a chore or homework, or as a signal to show that
something is not worthy of time or energy. These days,
as is often the case with fleeting popular-culture catch-
phrases, you'll rarely see the "W" brandished, though
the dismissive "whatever" is still muttered.

Region: From the United States, where it originated, this gesture spread to areas with a high permeation of Western film culture.

Environment: In its heyday, the whatever gesture was used willy-nilly in shopping malls, high school halls, and prom-like balls. Movie theaters, diners, and suburban homes were overrun with finger-spelled "whatevers." These are still the spots to see the rare throwback usage of this gesture, sometimes used ironically.

Execution: 1. **Raise both arms above the chest, just below the face.**

2. **Bring your hands together, palms out.**

3. **Drop the outer three fingers of each hand, leaving the thumb and index finger extended.**

4. **Bring your hands together until they meet at the thumbs, forming a large "W" in the air. You may overlap the nails of your thumbs, cross your thumbs entirely, or simply touch the edges together.**

5. **Solidly pump the "W" into the air in front of you, establishing it in space [Fig. A].**

6. Say or mouth "whatever." If you speak it aloud, it is best to emphasize the second syllable.

7. For added emphasis, tilt your head to one side and roll your eyes (see ROLL OF THE EYES, page 76).

FIG. A

Variations of Performance:	Less popularly, and using only one hand, the "W" may be formed with the first three fingers extended.

  YAWN

Usage and Origins:	*The mouth is opened wide.* Whether done intentionally or as a reflex, the yawn usually means the same thing, though only the deliberate and pointed yawn should be taken as an insulting or disapproving gesture.

The yawn is the universal expression of tiredness or boredom and whether it is real or fake, if another sees it, he is liable to "catch" the yawn and yawn himself. Medical experts generally believe that reflexive yawns occur because of low levels of oxygen in our lungs, while the mock yawn gesture shows supreme disinterest in what someone is saying, or even in his very presence. The message behind a performed yawn is "You're such a bore," or "I'd rather do anything other than pay attention to you."

Region:
Because cures for exhaustion and boredom have yet to be found, you'll see this gesture in both its real and fake forms throughout the world.

Yawning without covering your mouth is considered impolite in many countries, including the United States, Canada, and most of Western Europe. In Japan and Korea, as well as other Asian countries, any open-mouthed gesture is considered rude.

Environment:
Classical music concerts, school classrooms, libraries, and ballets will see a fair amount of yawning by disinterested participants. Any vessel used for long trips, from an SUV to a Learjet, will see passengers in the throes of yawning. Finally, boredom can strike even in seemingly exciting places, so don't be surprised to see the rare yawn at an ice hockey game, a rock concert, or a lively evening out with friends.

Execution: 1. Open your mouth wide.

2. Squint.

3. Inhale heavily, but with little noise.

4. Exhale, with as much noise and fanfare as is deemed appropriate.

5. Cover your mouth with one hand, palm facing in, if politeness or exaggeration is desired.

IV. Mating

39. **ARM AROUND**

Usage and Origins:

One arm is placed around the waist or shoulders of a companion. This casual gesture, the "half-embrace," is one of the more basic signs of affection or comfort, showing loving or tender feelings toward another person. Usually, the configuration calls for the taller person, generally the man, to put his arm around the shorter person, often the woman. This is not a hard-and-fast rule, however. In many cases, the shorter person will counter with an arm around the other's waist.

This is a gesture that occurs both while walking and while standing still, but caution should be used when walking with an arm around another, as this gesture has been known to slow progress.

The kind of affection conveyed by the arm around gesture is often that of lovers, though friends can and do employ this gesture in equal measure. In non-mating circumstances, it can be a "buddy" gesture and may be about as close and intimate as macho men will get. It is one of the only ways many men (especially in Western cultures) will perform continual physical contact with another man.

Additionally, a parent may tenderly put an arm around a child to show affection or to comfort.

Region: Putting an affectionate or consoling arm around a friend or lover is something that is done all over the world, both in private and in public. Be cautious when using this gesture with the opposite sex in areas of the Middle East, such as Saudi Arabia, where public displays of affection are against the law.

Environment: Both comfort and affection are shown in all localities. It is common for lovers to show affection in this way in a variety of places, from the supermarket to the sidewalk in town.

    When a child is hurt on the playground or awakes from a disturbing dream, his mother or father will put an arm around him to make him feel better, and when a player makes a good play, her teammates will throw their arms around her in excitement and congratulations as they walk off the field.

Execution: 1. **Extended one arm out to one side.**

    2. **Place your arm across the shoulders of another person.**

    3. **Squeeze the other person to your side gently.**

Variations of Performance: You may put an arm around another's waist, rest your hand on his back or backside, or put your hand in his back pocket; both partners may half-embrace one another.

---

40. 📷 **EYEBROW WIGGLE**

Usage and
Origins:

The eyebrows are raised and lowered in quick succession.
At the beginning of the twentieth century, the eyebrow wiggle gesture was a risqué way for a man to let a woman know of his attraction to her. In the Marx Brothers movies of the first half of the twentieth century, Groucho would often wiggle his eyebrows as a joke, and from there the gesture became more a comic cliché than a come-on.

The eyebrow wiggle gesture is often used in the West as an indication to a friend that someone may be interested in her, as if to say "this dork is eyeing you!" In this context, it may be paired with the rolling of the eyes gesture (see page 76).

A person may wiggle his eyebrows at the object of his affection, though rarely when intimacy with that person is not already established. Though used facetiously in many countries, in most Arab countries the eyebrow wiggle gesture is part of normal flirtation.

Region:

You will see the eyebrow wiggle in all regions around the globe, but the meaning will be different depending on where you are, as described above.

Environment: A man might wiggle his eyebrows at a woman who is across a crowded living room or bar, just to let her know he has lascivious plans for later in the evening. A person might employ the eyebrow wiggle gesture on a street to let another know he is romantically interested.

Execution: 1. **Raise your eyebrows.**

2. **Lower your eyebrows.**

3. **Repeat rapidly several times.**

4. **Smile.**

Variations of Performance: The "eyebrow flash" is an unconscious greeting practiced by everyone. It happens very quickly, in one-third of a second, and is accompanied by a smile. It is just a shorter version of the wiggle and is a typical friendly greeting among all humans.

41.   **EYELID FLUTTER**

Usage and Origins: *The eyes are widened slightly and then opened and closed rapidly.* The eyelid flutter has sexist connotations, and for good reason. This is a gesture that is commonly practiced by young women in order to show that they are wide-eyed and innocent, in an act of obvious subterfuge.

You will rarely if ever see a man bat his eyelashes, except as an exaggerated protestation of innocence. It is generally invoked by women who want something or would like to be excused from a particular wrong or offensive action they have committed.

Region: Eyelid fluttering is most often practiced in the Western world. In Taiwan and Hong Kong, repeatedly blinking the eyes at someone is considered impolite.

Environment: All areas of suburban homes will see this gesture in action, from the backyard to the bedroom, and anywhere else a wayward woman seeks the forgiveness of her man.

Execution: 1. **Tilt your head slightly upward.**

2. **While looking up slightly, rapidly close and open your eyes.**

3. **Smile.**

42. 📷 **HAIR FLIP**

Usage and
Origins:

A female tosses her hair to call attention to its beauty.
The hair flip is often an unconscious courting
action—a gesture used mainly by women to gain the
attention of a love interest. In many instances, women
might flip their hair on purpose to accomplish the
same goal. This gesture works best with shiny, healthy
hair, though the length doesn't particularly matter; as
long as it can swing about, the hair can be flipped.

You may choose to flip your hair behind your
shoulder by tossing your head, or you may flip it
with your hand—either way, the person you're flirt-
ing with will generally respond positively.

Region:

The hair flip is used both consciously and unconsciously in regions all over the world where women's
hair can be left uncovered.

Environment:

Lovely ladies toss their locks to gain attention in a
variety of places—from parks to public pools to parties. Perhaps the best place to see this gesture in play
is at an outdoors affair, where shiny hair gleams in
the sunshine and will generate the most attention.

Execution:

1. **Make eye contact with your companion.**

2. Toss your head so that your hair falls behind your shoulders, or so that it moves in the air.

or

1. Make eye contact with your companion.

2. Raise one hand to touch your hair.

3. Use your hand to lift and throw your hair away from your face.

4. Shake your head for effect.

43. **HOLDING HANDS**

Usage and Origins:

The hands of two people are clasped together. Hand-holding first occurs when babies are learning to walk and will grab onto most anything to stay upright—often a parent's hand. As a child grows older, she will hold a parent or caretaker's hand as she crosses the street or when in the midst of a large crowd, so as to not get lost or separated from the adult.

From these simple origins, the natural bond between a parent and child that is shown with hand-holding evolved into a gesture of affection that carries over into romantic relationships.

Lovers will often hold hands as a mutual gesture of loving feelings; because both partners are equal participants holding one another's hand, this gesture usually lacks any kind of power play unless one person is holding the other's hand in order to pull him in a certain direction or otherwise control him. It is sometimes used between friends as well as lovers and connotes tender feelings and the desire to touch one another.

Region: Hand-holding is common practice between parent and child, lovers, and friends throughout the world.

In the Middle East, it is not unusual for male friends to hold hands without any implied sexual meaning, while in the West, this is less common.

Be cautious when using this gesture with the opposite sex in areas of the Middle East, such as Saudi Arabia, where public displays of affection are against the law.

Environment: You are likely to see a parent holding a child's hand at a parade, while crossing a busy intersection, or while walking in the park. Lovers hold hands in a variety of places, from the movie theater to the beach to across the table at a restaurant. Since holding hands is intimate yet generally accepted as a public display of affection, you are likely to see it most anywhere.

Execution:	The holding hands gesture requires two people.

1. **Reach out to another person.**

2. **Grasp the hand nearest you in your hand.**

Variations of Performance:	You may wish to interlock your fingers with the fingers of the other person.

44. **KISS KISS**

Usage and Origins:	*The lips are puckered and the air is kissed, making audible sounds.* Similar to air kisses (see page 21) yet employed for differrent reasons, the kiss kiss gesture is used in order to gain the attention of passers-by, or to call a person or animal over to you.

Usually, men call out to beautiful women with the kiss kiss gesture in a wide variety of places around the world. This is not necessarily socially acceptable, nor is it likely to glean the kind of results these men probably have in mind.

Additionally, the kiss kiss gesture is also used by pet owners to call their furry friends, often accompanied by the words "here, kitty, kitty, kitty." This meaning will generally be inoffensive, except to those who find it disgustingly saccharine to make kissing noises at an animal.

Region: When used to gain attention or call someone to you, this gesture is used around the world. In Mexico, the kiss kiss gesture is used to call a waiter over to the table, and in the Philippines, it is the way in which street vendors try to lure customers to them.

Environment: A woman may find herself being kiss kissed as she walks down the street, through a restaurant, or anywhere else men might notice her. Pets are called with this gesture in homes, parks, and on beaches.

In Mexico, the kiss kiss gesture will be seen additionally in restaurants, bars, and cafes. And in the Philippines, outdoor bazaars will see their share of the kiss kiss gesture in use.

Execution: 1. **Purse the lips.**

2. **Following the directions outlined in Kiss (see page 19), kiss the air directly in front of the face with rapid-fire intensity.**

45.   📷   **LICKING OF THE LIPS**

Usage and   *The tongue is slowly run over the lips to entice a*
Origins: *potential mate.* Some anthropologists believe that wetting the lips, or making them look slick with lipstick or gloss, is an act set forth to mimic the look of

female genitalia, therefore drawing in a proper mate. Strange, then, that the biggest proponent of lip-licking is the average adolescent boy, who will practice this gesture in hopes of enticing a teenage girl to kiss him.

In other contexts, the licking of the lips gesture is used extensively in blockbuster, male-centric films; generally an overtly attractive woman wearing a short, tight, red dress is shown seductively licking her lips at the male protagonist across a bar/highway/counter/table.

Regardless of who's licking their lips, there is little question as to the intent of the gesture: the slow tongue over the lips is so reminiscent of kissing that there should be no misunderstanding as to what is meant.

Region: : The licking of the lips gesture is used to generate that come-hither vibe in North and South America.

Environment: : School dances, hallways, cafeterias, and classrooms will see their share of teenagers licking their lips in an attempt to assuage hormonal urges. Crowded bars, restaurants, and parties are spaces in which adults may lick their lips in an attempt to assuage their own hormonal urges.

Execution: : 1. **Extend your tongue out of your mouth, off to one side.**

2. Lick the upper lip, starting at one side and ending at the other [FIG. A].

3. Continue around the corner of the mouth.

4. Lick your bottom lip and pull your tongue back into your mouth [FIG. B].

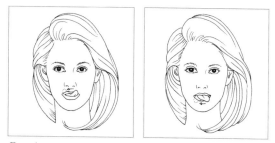

FIG. A   FIG. B

46. **THE SIZZLE**

Usage and
Origins:

The forefinger is quickly licked and held in the air, after which a hissing noise is made with the teeth and tongue, as if to suggest that the finger has touched something hot. This is a gesture whose origins are no mystery; the sound accompanying it—like putting meat on a barbecue—says it all. When something, or, more likely, someone, is particularly attractive (often called "hot" in modern vernacular) and it must be pointed out, this is the gesture to use. Whether gesturing to a known or unknown person, or in seriousness or jest, your meaning will be clear.

Likewise, outside of mating practices, this gesture is often done by a person in reference to herself, as in, "I did great on that exam, I'm on fire!"

Sometimes, the finger that has been licked might be used to actually touch the person or thing deemed hot or fantastic—at other times, it can be only pointed in the general direction.

Region: This is a largely Western gesture and will be seen most often in the United States, with possible usage in Europe and other areas where American culture has exerted its influence.

Environment: A rowdy bar or club is a good place to put this gesture to use. High school hallways and college campuses see their share of this gesture at exam time, and virtually any place where bathing suits are worn and therefore attractive bodies are on display—from pools to dockside restaurants—will see this gesture in use.

Execution: 1. **Make a fist** [FIG. A].

           2. **Extend your index finger** [FIG. B].

3. Bring the finger to your mouth.

4. Touch the tip of your finger to your tongue. (If you are uncomfortable doing so, mimicking this action is also acceptable.)

5. Bring the finger away from your mouth and toward whatever it is that you think is hot. (Sometimes when the gesturer believes that she is "hot" she will place her finger on her hip or butt.) If gesturing about something intangible or untouchable, leave the finger in the air.

6. Say "tsssssss."

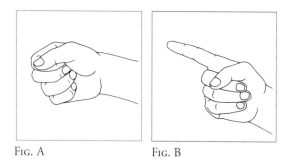

FIG. A   FIG. B

Variations of Performance:	In Italy and other parts of Europe, men will quickly shake their whole hand in front of their bodies to flirt

with women they find attractive, miming the action of cooling the fingers after touching something hot (presumably, the woman).

Another similar gesture is the Syrian thumb bite, in which a man bites his thumb and then shakes it as though he were in pain to symbolize the pain that a man feels because a woman is not paying attention to him.

On the television series *Laverne & Shirley*, the characters Lenny and Squiggy often employed a similar gesture whenever they glimpsed an attractive woman. Since they knew they had no chance of associating with beautiful women because of their extreme social dysfunction, they bit the heels of their fists in frustrated desire.

47. **THE STARE**

Usage and Origins:
To look at someone steadily and intently. The stare is a gesture that is frequently used as either a flirtation device or a threatening one. A lascivious, lingering glance expresses sexual threat, or—less menacing and more common—shows interest on the part of the one doing the staring. Perhaps the initiator of the stare will engage the object to stare back; this is then called "eye contact," and may show mutual sexual interest.

As a threatening gesture, the stare hints at attack, and the person being stared at will become increasingly uncomfortable. The stare is threatening across cultures and indeed in the animal kingdom—primates use the stare as a warning gesture as well.

Hopefully, the person and the situation will determine whether the stare is flirtatious or menacing, and the object of the stare will respond accordingly.

Region: The stare is used worldwide, both to express sexual interest and to warn of an impending attack.

Environment: Staring knows no locality; since it may not be noticed by the subject of the gaze, starers are generally free to stare anywhere without making spectacles of themselves. Watch for stares at bars, restaurants, malls, sporting events, or on bustling city streets.

Execution: 1. **Turn your head to face another person.**

2. **Fix both eyes on your subject.**

3. **Do not look away and do not blink.**

4. **Continue looking at your subject. The duration is up to you.**

5. **Look away.**

Variations of
Performance:

A very effective, flirtatious variation of the stare is the sidelong glance. To perform this gesture, do not face your companion directly; look sideways at your target with your head lowered to show coyness. This stare, used all over the world, is a contradiction, as the glance is bold while the head is lowered shyly.

48. **THE WINK**

Usage and
Origins:

One eye is closed and then quickly opened again. The wink is a gesture that can have many meanings, with the flirtatious implication probably the most cartoonish. Anthropologists postulate that the wink gesture suggests a private secret: The closed eye is symbolically keeping the secret while the open eye is excluding others from it.

The wink gesture today is a sign of a shared secret, either between friends as an act of collusion or between potential lovers as an act of future intimacy. It is easy to see how the wink gesture became an indicator of sexual attraction; through the use of gesture, you are nonverbally saying "I like you, you like me."

These days, the wink is often practiced as a funny, exaggerated signal of romantic interest, generally best used with someone you already know, as flashing a wink at a stranger is not usually welcomed. This is because, unfortunately, the wink gesture has taken on meanings of sleaziness and a too-forward aggressiveness that connotes not romance, but slimy insincerity.

Region: Winking is used as a form of flirtation in the United States, but it is better to avoid it outside North America. It is improper to wink in Australia and it is impolite in parts of the Far East, such as Hong Kong.

Environment: Due to the somewhat subtle nature of the wink, it will be seen in a variety of locales. High-school hallways may see their share of this gesture, as will parks, shops, and smoky bars and clubs. You might even catch the errant wink at the office.

Execution: If you find that closing one eye causes that side of your face to scrunch up unpleasantly, try the other eye. The ideal wink involves no motion by any part of your face but your one eye.

1. **Close an eye.**

2. **After a second or less, open it again. It's best to keep the duration of the wink brief.**

Variations of Performance: Most winks should show no other facial movement but that of the eye, but when the wink is used as an exaggerated joke, the whole face is involved. Sometimes a smile or other gesture may accompany the wink.

V. Offensive and Profane

49. 📷 **CHIN FLICK**

Usage and
Origins:

The fingernails of one hand are brushed under and away from the chin in a continuous motion. The chin flick is a gesture that has several meanings, all of which are certainly negative and some that are quite insulting. The chin flick gesture represents a symbolic beard flip (in France, this gesture is known as *la barbe*, or "the beard"), and it is used to express supreme disinterest.

Its meanings are variable—from "Get lost" to "Shut up" to "Under no circumstances will I put up with you anymore" to "You are boring." It is in this latter context that the gesture's meaning is more evident: "You have been talking so long that my beard has grown while I've been listening to you."

In southern Italy, you'll find men using this gesture as a means of saying "no" from a distance, as in "There are no parking spaces left in the lot, so don't pull in here."

In some cultures, this gesture carries with it a more disrespectful connotation. While the meaning is not clearly defined, it translates roughly to "Get the fuck away from me!" It is a gesture that gets children in serious trouble with adults and is responsible for countless fights among peers.

Region: As a gesture of disinterest, the chin flick gesture is common in French-speaking nations, as well as in northern Italy and the former Yugoslavia. As a simple way to express negative feelings, it is used in southern Italy and the Italian islands. You'll see this gesture used insultingly in Tunisia, and, rarely, in North America and the British Isles.

Environment: The chin flick gesture is like many insulting or offensive gestures in that it will not be used nearly as much as one might like to use it, due to rules of propriety and manners. However, you may see the chin flick gesture during a boring lecture in France or just before a street fight in Tunisia.

A particularly famous incidence of the chin flick gesture occurs in the film *Grease* as part of Rizzo's song "Look at me, I'm Sandra Dee." Sandy is so horrified at the insult that she bursts into tears.

Execution: 1. Touch the top of your neck, along the bottom of your chin, with the back of the fingertips of one hand. Your fingers will make a relaxed 45- to 90-degree angle with the rest of your hand and forearm, palm facing in.

2. Drag your fingertips along the base of your chin [FIG. A].

3. When you reach the end of your chin, flick your fingers into the air [Fig. B].

4. Spread your fingers slightly and hold them in the air in front of your face for less than one second.

5. Drop your hand.

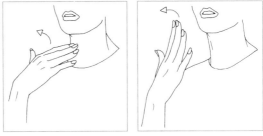

Fig. A   Fig. B

Variations of Performance: Increase the intensity of the insult or disinterest by repeating the flicking motion.

50. **CROTCH GRAB**

Usage and Origins: *A man loosely grabs his own genitals in one hand and shakes them.* If you are a man, it's tough to find a more offensive and insulting gesture to perform.

Indeed, you'll rarely see women enacting the crotch grab gesture though there was a brief period in the mid-1990s when pop-sensation Madonna attempted to claim the gesture as a strongly feminist one and used it to express herself in music video. This is an extreme exception, however, as the act of actually shaking the genitals at another is quite obviously impossible for those without penises.

The gesture itself has two insulting layers: First, disrespect is expressed by the fact that the gesturer thinks so little of the recipient of the gesture that he will perform the intimate act of touching his genitals in public without embarrassment. The second part is very simple: It means "Up yours!" and draws attention to the appropriate part of the anatomy to enact this insult.

Region: The crotch grab gesture is most common in Central America (especially Mexico) and the United States.

Environment: Due to the very disrespectful attitude that this gesture conveys, it will hopefully not be directed at you very often. A rude man might enact the crotch grab gesture in a bar or at a rowdy sporting event, where alcohol flows freely and reduces any sense of propriety.

Additionally, this is a very common pose to see in Michael Jackson's videos, where it is not an insult so much as a dance step, for reasons unknown.

Execution:

1. Place one hand over your crotch.

2. Bend your knees and arch your back slightly to make your crotch area more prominent.

3. Cup your fingers under your crotch and make a squeezing motion once.

4. For a finishing flourish, shake your hand from side to side slightly while still holding your crotch.

Variations of Performance:

In Argentina, a gesture with the same meaning is performed when a man uses both hands to slap and grab his own inner thighs. For a woman to express the same sentiment, she may lift one of her breasts; this is very rarely performed.

51. 📷 **CUNNILINGUS**

Usage and Origins:

The forefinger and middle finger are splayed and raised to the face in front of the mouth; the tongue peeks through and wiggles about, imitating the act of cunnilingus. The cunnilingus gesture is clearly profane but will seldom be used in a disrespectful way to hurt or insult another person. It is more commonly a way to refer to an act that is somewhat taboo and creates embarrassment when it is talked about, or to shock someone with its overt bawdiness. It is rare to see this gesture outside of particularly silly rock 'n' roll videos or amongst giggling girlfriends who may be shy to talk about such an intimate act.

As with all overtly profane gestures, performing this one publicly is against the law in some more-proper areas of the United States. It will certainly earn you a detention in any middle or high school in the country, and if directed toward a female teacher, you may find yourself suspended.

If a man or woman flashes this gesture at a woman, it might be interpreted as a sexual suggestion or request, albeit a rude and clumsy one. The woman may choose to respond with interest or with disgust and anger— whatever suits her fancy.

Region: This gesture will rarely be seen outside of Western regions, where, while still somewhat taboo in conversation, oral sex is openly—and often disrespectfully— discussed.

Environment: Slumber parties and music videos from the early 1990s are the best places to see this gesture shyly and cartoonishly performed, respectively. Sexually open television series, such as *Sex and the City*, will make use of this gesture, as will kids and young adults who want to provoke others into embarrassed shock.

Execution: 1. Make a fist with one hand.

2. Extend your index and middle fingers.

3. Splay apart the extended fingers to form a "V."

4. Turn your hand so that your palm faces your body.

5. Raise the "V" so that its base rests on your chin.

6. Stick your tongue through the "V" made by your fingers.

7. Wiggle your tongue.

---

52. **FELLATIO**

Usage and
Origins:

The tongue is pushed against the cheek in a closed mouth so that it forces the cheek to protrude. Used to imitate what the face looks like while in the act of fellatio, this gesture has much the same insulting yet silly interpretation as its female counterpart, the cunnilingus gesture (see page 111), though it is more commonly used. This may be because fellatio is a more acceptable sexual act to discuss and therefore, to make fun of.

It is used most often by pre-teens to naughtily refer to the sexual act in order to embarrass their peers or as a joke. The fellatio gesture is often evoked in middle-school settings, such as the cafeteria or playground, to spread rumors that some young woman is "easy" because she performs fellatio.

Region: This gesture will rarely be seen outside of Western regions.

Environment: Places where adolescents gather, such as malls, school hallways, and diners, are common areas to see this gesture in use amidst much giggling. College campuses may be a venue for the performance of this gesture, since it is here where the battle for maturity is fought and often not quite won.

Execution:
1. **With your mouth closed, move the tip of your tongue over to one side of the inside of your mouth.**

2. **Push your tongue into your cheek from the inside, making the cheek puff out slightly.**

3. **Repeat if desired, for emphasis.**

Variations of Performance: In a variation of this gesture, you might move one hand, closed into a fist as if holding an erect penis, in rhythm with the tongue to further accentuate the gesture.

53. 📷 **THE FIG**

Usage and
Origins:

The hand is closed in a fist, with the tip of the thumb protruding between the knuckles of the index and middle fingers. The fig gesture dates back to antiquity, and while there is widespread speculation as to the origin and meaning of the name, there is no agreement among experts and therefore no definitive answer. Historians also disagree about the exact origin of the gesture, but most speculate that it is a reference to female genitalia.

There is evidence to suggest that the fig gesture was used in ancient Greece to break magic spells. For this reason, its likeness was used on good-luck amulets worn around the neck to ward off the evil eye and in artwork. It was thought that an overt sexual display would distract the evil spirit from committing destruction. This ancient meaning of the gesture still exists—to this day, people in Portuguese-speaking nations wear amulets in the shape of a hand performing the fig gesture as good luck charms.

The sexual origins of the gesture have been lost in some cultures. Today, the most widespread and common interpretation and use of this gesture is as an imitation of the act of copulation, in which the thumb represents a penis and the fingers represent labia.

The meaning expressed behind the gesture varies across Europe and the Americas, but it is usually interpreted either as a sexual proposition or as an insult, depending on region and context (see below).

Region: In Belgium, Holland, Denmark, and Germany, the fig gesture is a sexual comment that means "I would like to have sex with you." In France, Greece, and Turkey, it is more of a sexual insult, as in "Up yours." In Portugal and Brazil, this gesture is still a good luck charm that is represented on jewelry.

In the United States, the fig gesture is not used as a particularly offensive or even insulting gesture; it is usually only evoked in a child's game in which someone pretends to grab the nose off another's face and hold it between the fingers to mean "I've got your nose." This game is also played throughout most of Europe.

Environment: Places where things become chaotic and tasteless due to alcohol consumption, such as bars, parties, or carnivals, are likely spots to see the fig gesture in use, whether as insult or an invitation to sexual activity.

In Portugal and Brazil, the fig will be seen worn around the neck at sporting events and anywhere else good luck or protection is desired. Remember that here it carries no insulting connotation.

Execution: 1. **Begin to make a fist with one hand.**

2. **Instead of setting your thumb across your fingers, tuck it between the index and middle fingers, near the knuckles so that just the pad of the thumb is exposed.**

3. **Hold out your fist at mid-torso.**

4. **Shake your fist back and forth slightly.**

54. **THE FINGER**

Usage and Origins:

The middle finger is extended while the other fingers are pressed into a fist. Anthropologists contend that the finger gesture has been in use for more than 2,000 years. The Romans called it *"digitus impudicus"* or "indecent digit," and there are countless references to it in writings by classical authors. It translates to "fuck you," and the most obvious origin of this insulting and obscene meaning is the gesture's resemblance to a phallus, with the middle finger as the erect penis and the tucked-under fingers as testicles.

Despite its beginnings as a phallic-symbol insult, it has evolved into one of the more widespread displays of anger and insolence and has lost much of its sexual meaning. It can even be a playful or humorous insult, especially when it is flashed in a seemingly innocent way, as when one scratches one's head or points to something using the middle finger. It is unclear why Americans often refer to performing the finger gesture as "flipping the bird."

Region: The finger gesture has made its way around the world and can be seen everywhere these days. (There are analogous gestures in other countries, such as Britain's use of the "V" gesture; see page 227). Use of this gesture is more prevalent in the United States than anywhere else.

Environment: Since people lose their tempers in an endless variety of locales, it is difficult to pinpoint specific spots that will see an increased use of the finger gesture. Road rage could be the leading catalyst for the gesture, so highways or roads will see an abundance of extended middle fingers.

Execution:
1. Make a fist with one hand, palm facing in.

2. Raise the middle finger of this hand. Extend the finger as straight up in the air as possible.

3. Hold the hand up in the air, at face-level.

4. Jerk your hand once.

Variations of
Performance:

You may hold your arm and finger still or you may jerk it in the air, as directed above. Some people will slap their other hand against the crook of their elbow as they make the gesture [Fig. A].

In Arab nations, the same gesture is performed by splaying out the fingers, palm down, with the middle finger pointing straight down. In Lebanon and Syria, the back of a closed fist, with knuckles facing up, is brought quickly toward the open palm of the other hand, with the middle finger popping out of the fist at the moment of impact. This implies a violent sexual act such as a rape and adds a slapping noise to the gesture.

Finally, Russians bend back the middle finger of one hand using the forefinger of the other hand. This is called "looking under the cat's tail" and expresses the same meaning as giving the finger gesture as directed in "Execution."

Fig. A

55. **LIMP WRIST**

Usage and Origins:
The hand is raised and held slack at the wrist. The limp wrist is an insulting gesture that implies a man is gay. In previous centuries, tight sleeves were popular in women's fashion, so women could only gesture from the wrist down. This made any wrist movement awkward, and thus, the flaccid, flapping wrist is associated with effeminacy.

This gesture is not seen as often in the twenty-first century; it experienced its heyday in the mid-1980s, when being accused of homosexuality held more of a stigma than it does today. Many men may still balk at the limp wrist if it is flashed their way, but as time passes it is possible that fewer people will evoke this gesture as an insult.

Region:
The limp wrist gesture is generally only seen in Western countries.

Environment:
Used fairly openly in public places during less "politically correct" times, this is a gesture that will rarely be used publicly today. You may catch a glimpse of it in a bar, frat house, or anywhere one might wish to indicate on the sly that someone is gay or joke that a friend is homosexual.

Color Plates

1. blown kiss

2. the bow

3a. fist-chest pound

3b. fist-chest pound

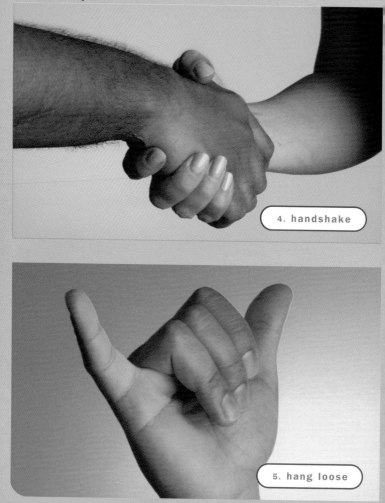

4. handshake

5. hang loose

6. hug

7. kiss

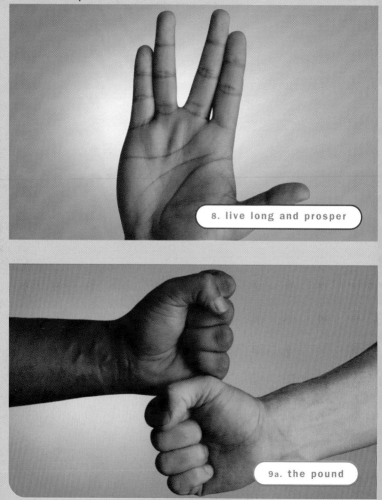

8. live long and prosper

9a. the pound

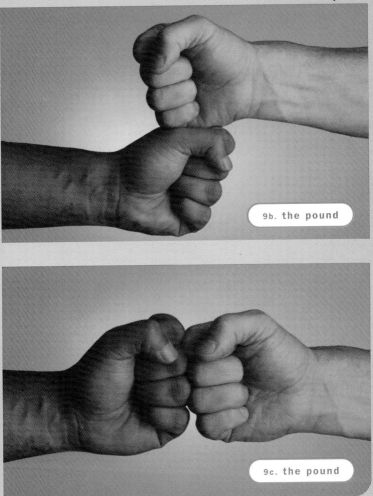

9b. the pound

9c. the pound

10. the salute

11. tip of the hat

12. waving

13a. applause

13b. applause

14. arms up

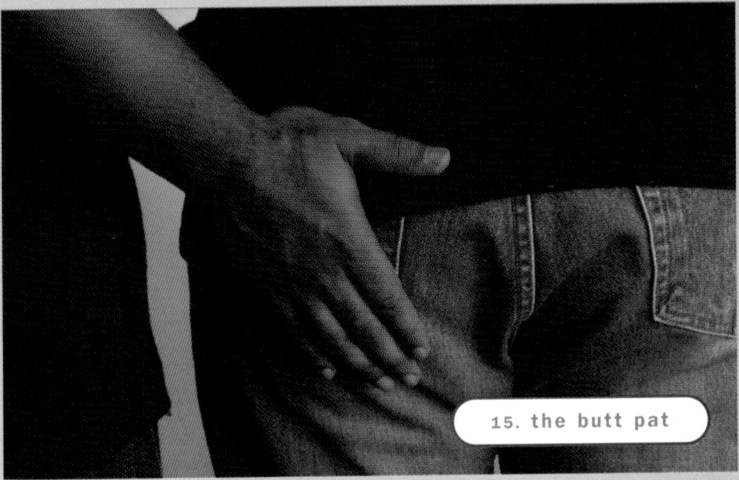

15. the butt pat

16. the high five

17a. nod "yes"

17b. nod "yes"

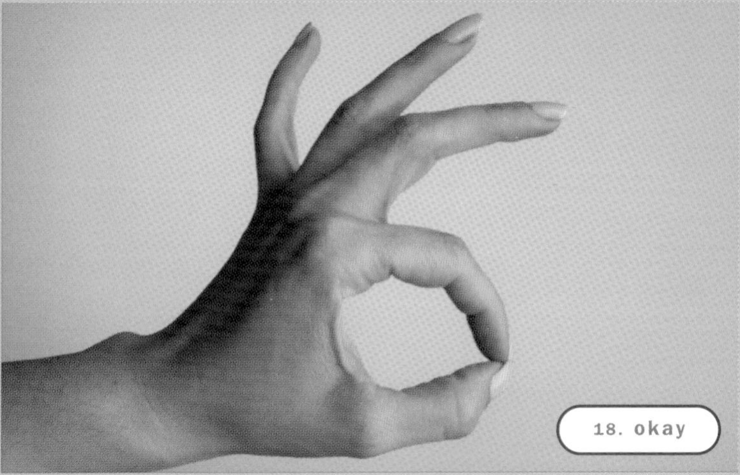

18. okay

19. raise the roof

20. smile

21. thumbs-up

22. the wave

23. arms akimbo

24. arms folded

25. the choke

26. eyebrow furrow

27. finger wag

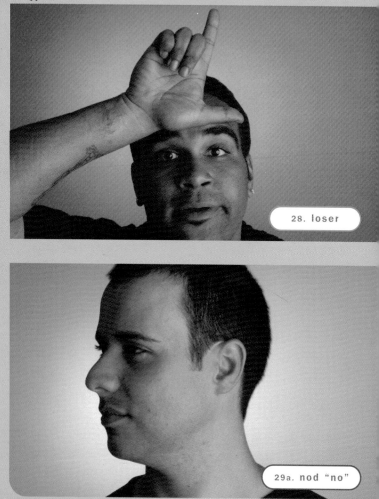

28. loser

29a. nod "no"

29b. nod "no"

30. nose hold

Disapproval

31. nose wrinkle

32. raspberry

33a. roll of the eyes

33b. roll of the eyes

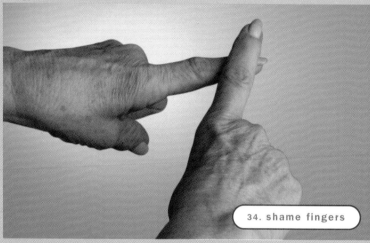

34. shame fingers

35. the spit

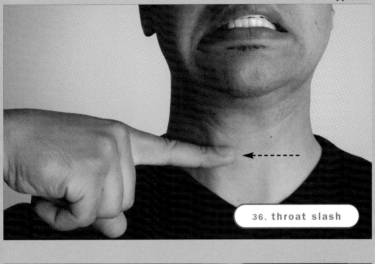

36. throat slash

37. whatever

38. yawn

39. arm around

40a. eyebrow wiggle

40b. eyebrow wiggle

41. eyelid flutter

42. hair flip

43. holding hands

44. kiss kiss

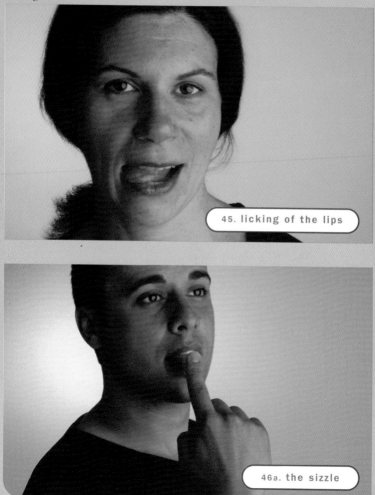

45. licking of the lips

46a. the sizzle

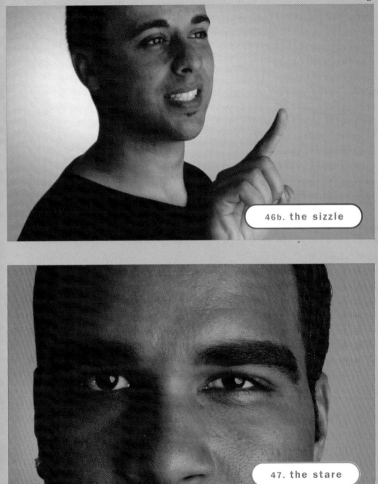

46b. the sizzle

47. the stare

48. the wink

49a. chin flick

49b. chin flick

50. crotch grab

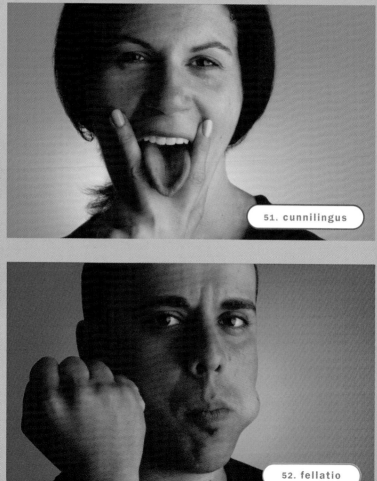

51. cunnilingus

52. fellatio

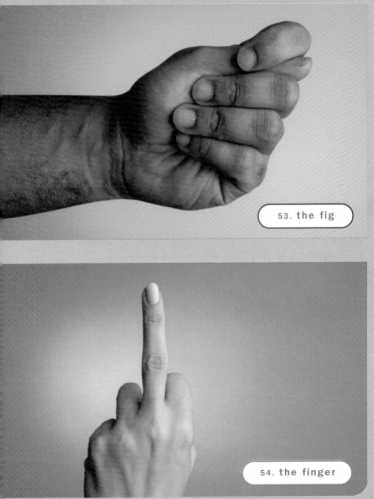

53. the fig

54. the finger

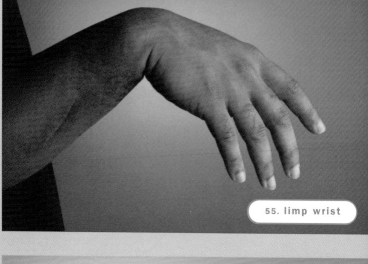

55. limp wrist

56. little penis

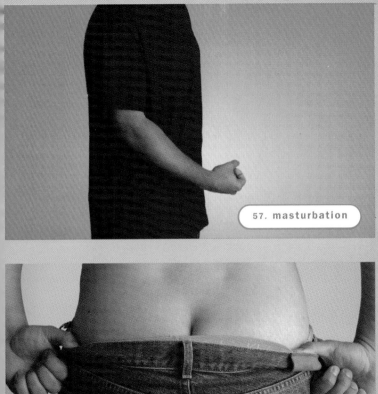

57. masturbation

58. the moon

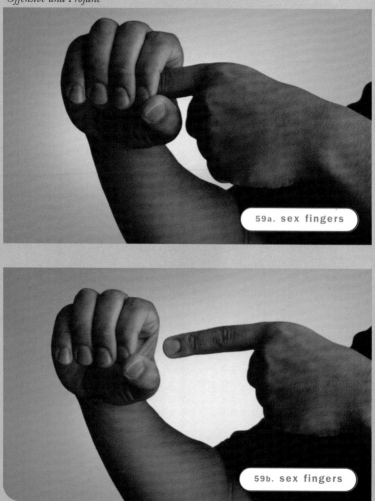

59a. sex fingers

59b. sex fingers

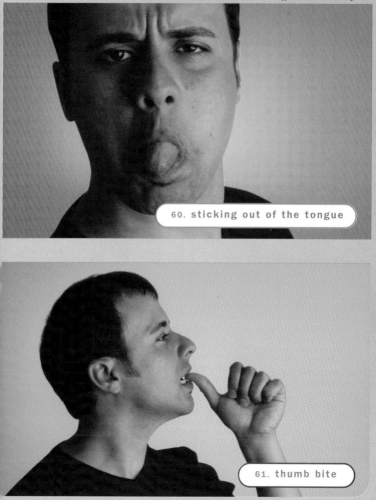

60. sticking out of the tongue

61. thumb bite

62. **thumbing of the nose**

63. **up yours**

64. "v" on the nose

65. busty

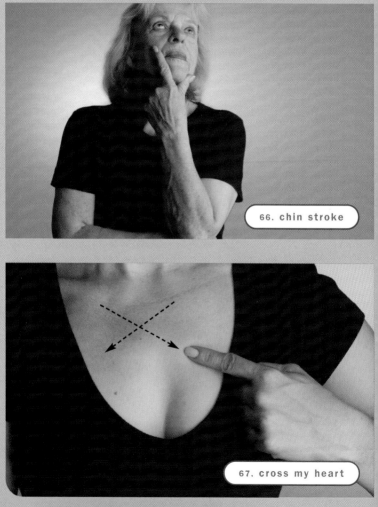

66. chin stroke

67. cross my heart

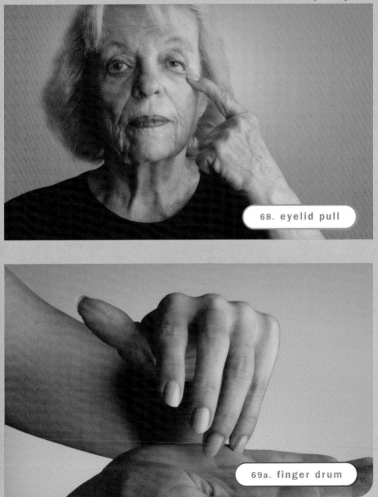

68. eyelid pull

69a. finger drum

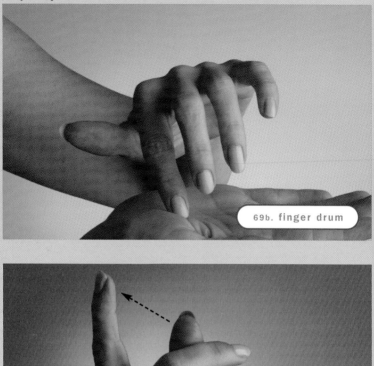

69b. finger drum

70. finger snap

71. fingernail buff

72. the fist

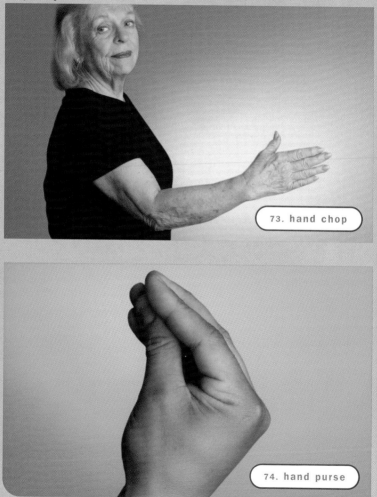

73. hand chop

74. hand purse

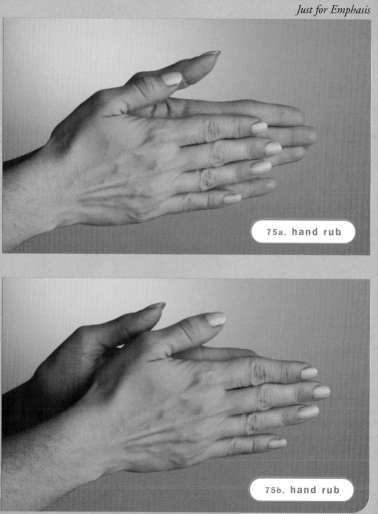

75a. hand rub

75b. hand rub

76. the horns

77. money

78. nose tap

79. one

80. the point

81. scratching of the head

82. shhh!

83. shocking!

84. the shrug

85. so-so

86. up to here

87. yadda yadda yadda

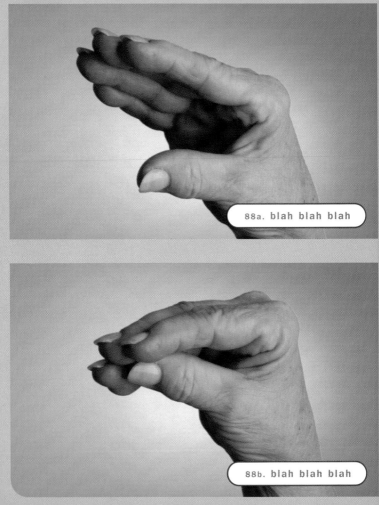

88a. blah blah blah

88b. blah blah blah

89. call me

90a. check please

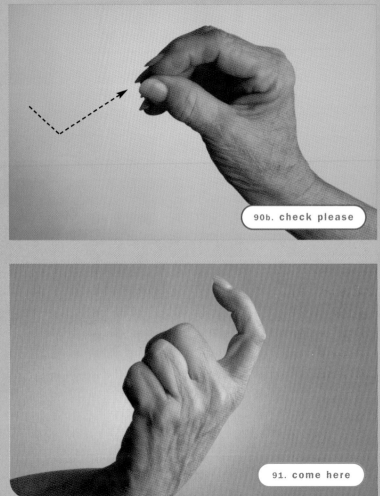

90b. check please

91. come here

92. crazy

93. duh!

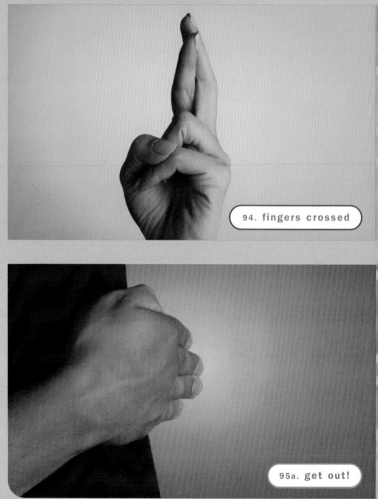

94. fingers crossed

95a. get out!

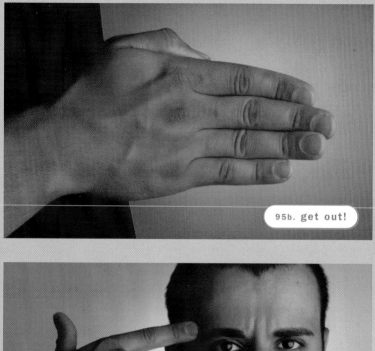

95b. get out!

96a. gun to head

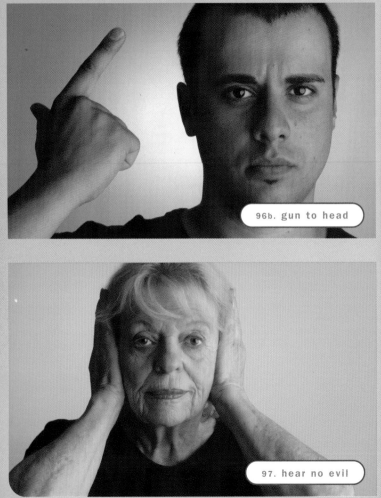

96b. gun to head

97. hear no evil

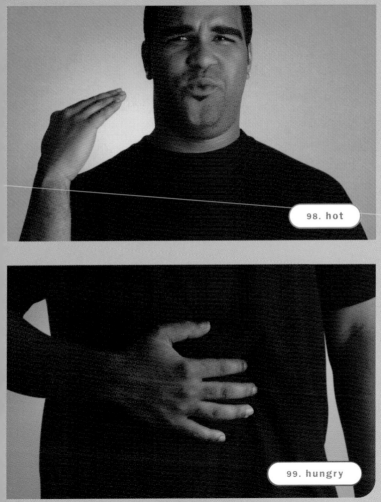

98. hot

99. hungry

100. let's drink

101a. pregnant

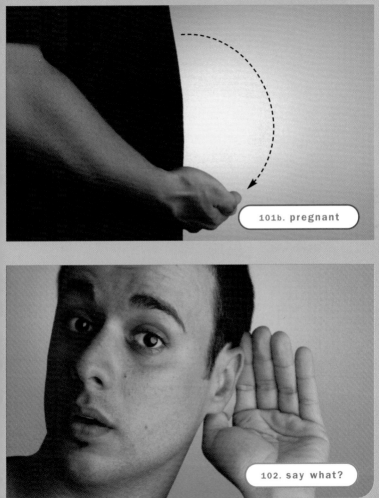

101b. pregnant

102. say what?

103. **smoking**

104. **stop**

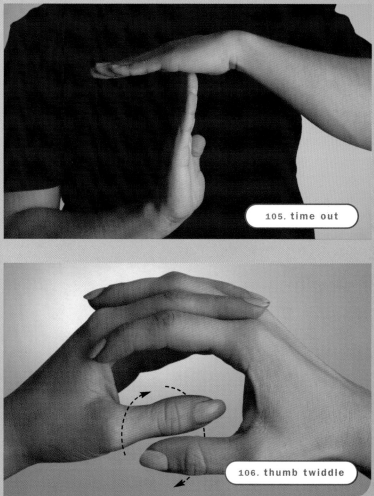

105. time out

106. thumb twiddle

107. the "v"

108. whoop-tee-do

Execution: 1. **Raise one hand to shoulder-level.**

2. **Let your wrist go limp.**

3. **For added effect, bob your wrist up and down a few times.**

Variations of Performance: Some people will perform this gesture with both hands.

56. 📷   **LITTLE PENIS**

Usage and Origins: *The pinkie finger is extended from a fist.* This is a popular gesture among women engaged in sharing secrets of sexual exploits in order to indicate a certain man's shortcoming. The pinkie is symbolic of the penis, but since the gesture employs the little finger and not one of the larger, more imposing fingers, this gesture insults the man who is being described by implying that he doesn't measure up.

If a woman is feeling particularly insulting toward a man, she might flash this gesture at him directly to let him know that she is, was not, or never could be sexually satisfied by him. Though men rarely, if ever, employ this gesture themselves, they do know what it means, and they will be sufficiently embarrassed by its use.

Region: As a sexual insult, this gesture is used all over the
            world but is most common in the Mediterranean. In
            Bali, the extended little finger means "bad," while the
            extended thumb means "good" (see THUMBS-UP,
            page 52), and does not always imply failure or success
            in the bedroom.

            In parts of Europe and South America, extending
            the pinkie to refer to a person implies thinness—one
            is so thin that he or she must be ill, or a woman is so
            skinny as to be considered unattractive. Here the ges-
            ture can be considered insulting, but not sexually.

Environment: Places where "girl talk" is common, such as coffee
            shops, restaurants, bars, and kitchens, are likely to see
            the most use of this gesture. A woman might insult a
            man virtually anywhere, though using this gesture in
            the bedroom or other sexual arena is certain to be
            extremely offensive to any man, so be cautious.

Execution: 1. **Hold one hand at a comfortable distance from
               your body.**

            2. **Make a loose fist.**

            3. **Extend your pinkie finger.**

            4. **You may wiggle the finger for emphasis, but it is
               not necessary.**

57. 📷 **MASTURBATION**

Usage and Origins:

The hand is held in a loose fist and shaken up and down in front of the body, just below the waist. Like many obscene gestures, this one mimes a sexual activity: male masturbation. In Britain, this gesture is often used by large crowds of spectators at football matches when a player on the opposite team makes a massive error, as if to say "You may as well have been masturbating for all the good that play did you."

In the United States, the masturbation gesture is performed to indicate disinterest or disbelief and it is used to accentuate a story or to insult someone behind his back. Loosely, the message is that the person being gestured to or about (usually a man—this gesture is rarely used toward women) may as well be masturbating for all the attention you're paying or for all the good it's doing him to say what he's saying.

It can also be used to imply that someone is being self-indulgent or self-centered.

Region:

This is a gesture you'll rarely see outside of the United States and parts of Europe.

Environment:

British football fans are reputed to be a rowdy lot, and they are likely to employ this gesture at matches or sports bars throughout the British Isles while watching a game. College campuses, urban office buildings, local taverns, and other spots where individuals tend to ramble on or exaggerate are common places to see this gesture used to indicate boredom, doubtfulness, or self-indulgence.

Execution: 1. **Slightly curl your fingers.**

2. **Hold your hand at waist-level.**

3. **Shake your hand back and forth, as if you were rolling dice.**

---

58.   **THE MOON**

Usage and Origins:

The trousers are briefly dropped, exposing the bare buttocks to a person or group of people. Mooning to insult is ancient in origin, and experts speculate that its roots are semi-religious. Centuries ago, believers supposed that the devil was extremely jealous of the curvy, symmetrical buttocks of humans, and they felt that showing him your naked backside would distract his evil-doing and protect against evil.

Additionally, Satan was believed to possess another face on his posterior; when the gesture was aimed toward others, it implied they were devil-worshippers. Though the anti-Satanic sentiment has been lost, the insolence of it has remained.

These days, mooning is often illegal, depending on whether or not the genitals are exposed in addition to the buttocks.

This insulting gesture is practiced far more often by men than by women; for women, the buttocks can sometimes be used to entice others to sexual feelings, while men usually display their rumps to offend.

Region: This gesture is largely confined to Europe and North America.

Environment: You are likely to see mooning at high school hangouts, on college campuses, in cars, at concerts, at sporting events, and especially in locations where alcohol is sold and/or consumed.

Adolescents on long bus excursions—perhaps field trips to historical locales—are the biggest proponent of the moon gesture, as to them, nothing is funnier or gives greater pleasure than appearing bare-assed for passing motorists.

Execution: 1. **Drop your trousers and undergarments** [Fig. A].

2. **Raise your shirt to fully expose the buttocks** [Fig. B].

3. **Bend over, taking care not to expose your frontal private parts.**

4. Aim the exposed buttocks at the object of mockery/derision. The posterior may be wiggled for emphasis.

5. Stand and replace trousers.

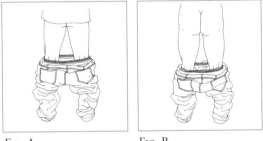

Fig. A   Fig. B

Variations of Performance: To be extra-offensive, the genitals can be exposed.

 59.   **SEX FINGERS**

Usage and Origins: *The forefinger is extended, inserted into a ring made by the other hand, and then pushed in and out quickly several times.* The symbolism of this gesture is so simple that it will not be lost on even the dullest individual: The ringed hand is the vagina, the opposite forefinger is the penis, and the action they perform together mimes intercourse.

Most children and pre-teens are fond of this gesture as a naughty way to talk about sex; they are intrigued by sexual matters, yet do not possess any understanding of them beyond the in-and-out motion. Since talking about sex with just about anyone is the most embarrassing thing to confront during childhood, often this gesture is mercifully used to indicate something sexual without words.

Region: The sex fingers gesture is used throughout Europe, the Americas, and the Middle East.

Environment: Since this gesture is a favorite with the under-13 set, it will be used throughout middle schools, from locker rooms to lunch tables, as well as on buses, at slumber parties, and on the playground.

Execution: 1. Make a fist with one hand [Fig. A].

2. Extend the index finger [Fig. B].

3. Make a fist with the other hand, keeping a slight space between the fingers and the palm.

4. Insert the index finger into the space between the fingers and the palm in the clenched hand.

5. Pull the index finger out.

6. Repeat several times.

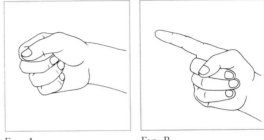

Fig. A   Fig. B

 STICKING OUT OF THE TONGUE

Usage and
Origins:

The tongue is protruded. This universal gesture originates in infancy, when a baby rejects food by naturally
sticking out her tongue. From childhood into adult-
hood, the gesture predictably evolves in meaning from
"I reject this food" to "I don't want you" and becomes
insulting.

Apart from its disdainful meaning, sticking the
tongue out is an unconscious gesture practiced when
an individual is concentrating very hard on a manual
task. This unconscious form of the gesture shows only

a slight protrusion, very different from the deliberate insult most often attributed to sticking out the tongue. Anthropologists believe that the sentiment implied in this instance is "Don't interrupt me," essentially an extension of the more obvious rejection discussed above. In this case, however, the gesture is not intentionally done to hurt or exclude another.

Region:
Both meanings are evoked with this gesture around the world, with one notable exception. In Tibet, people sometimes stick their tongues out to greet one another.

Environment:
This is an insult popular with children and will therefore be seen in elementary schools, on field trips, and at the playground.

As an unconscious gesture of concentration, the sticking out of the tongue gesture can be seen in garages all over the world, as people tinker with all manner of contraptions. It will also be seen in laboratories, operating rooms, and dentist's offices worldwide.

Execution:
1. **Open your mouth slightly.**

2. **Protrude your tongue out of your mouth until it is fully extended.**

3. **Keep your lips pursed against your tongue.**

Variations of
Performance:

In East Africa, this gesture is coupled with a right-handed throwing-away movement, and has the same insulting meaning.

In some Latin countries, the in-and-out motion of the tongue is considered very erotic and will be used to indicate sexual feelings or attraction.

In Lebanon, the protruded tongue moving from side to side is a disrespectful proposition from a man to a woman. Additionally, see the raspberry gesture (page 74).

61. **THUMB BITE**

Usage and
Origins:

The thumb is bitten gently and flicked away from the mouth. Considered by experts to be the Elizabethan equivalent of the finger gesture (see page 117), the thumb bite is a gravely insulting gesture. Though it is no longer included in the popular canon of gestures, it does make what is arguably the most famous appearance of a gesture in all of literature.

In Act I, Scene 1 of Shakespeare's *Romeo and Juliet*, Sampson of the Capulets bites his thumb at Abram of the Montagues, which causes the fight that ultimately leads to the tragic demise of the title characters.

While you won't see the thumb bite gesture practiced very often these days, literature buffs and historians may invoke it now and then as an allusion.

Region: You may experience the very occasional thumb bite
           in North America and Europe. In Syria, there is a
           gesture in which the thumb is bitten, but it does not
           carry the same meaning as the traditional thumb bite
           gesture. See THE SIZZLE, page 100.

Environment: Academic settings, such as libraries, lecture halls, and
                campus coffee houses may be the only spots to see this
                archaic gesture in use.

Execution: 1. Make a fist with one hand.

              2. Extend the tip of your thumb so that it is visible
                 above the fist.

              3. Bring your thumb to your mouth.

              4. Bite the tip of your thumb with your front teeth.

              5. Gently release your thumb and flick it toward
                 the object of your derision.

62. 📷   **THUMBING OF THE NOSE**

Usage and   *The hand is held erect, fingers splayed and wiggling,*
Origins: *with the tip of the thumb resting on the tip of the nose.*
             Thumbing the nose has the distinction of having

more names than any other gesture—14 in the English language alone and a wide variety in other languages. Some of its most common English monikers are cock a snook, pull a snook, cut a snook, make a long nose, take a sight, Queen Anne's fan, Japanese fan, Spanish fan, pull bacon, coffee-mill, and the five-fingered salute.

It is an ancient gesture that has fascinated historians for hundreds of years; there is half a millennium's worth of well-documented history but no definitive origin. There are at least seven different theories of the origin of the thumbing of the nose gesture, and though each arrives at a different specific beginning, none can be completely proven. The theorized origins include the deformed salute, a modification of thumb-sucking, a threat of snot-flicking, a grotesque nose, a phallic nose, a threatening cock's comb, or the implication of a bad smell or that someone stinks.

Though it has a variety of possible origins and at least twice as many names, there is no debate over the intention behind thumbing the nose: mockery and insult. Internationally, everyone knows the sentiment behind this gesture, and studies have shown that thumbing the nose is the most well-known gesture across Europe.

Region: Though it has many names in English and other languages, this gesture is recognized and causes offense the world over.

Environment: This is a gesture that is more likely to be employed by children than by adults and will therefore be seen most often in elementary schools, on playgrounds, in backyards, at sleep-away camps, and any other place where children interact with one another.

Adults may invoke this gesture as a playful childhood throwback, and when this happens, it will likely not be meant as an insult but rather as a gentle tease or even flirtation.

Execution: 1. **With your palm flat and your fingers splayed, place the end of your thumb to the tip of your nose.**

2. **Wiggle the extended fingers back and forth.**

3. **For emphasis, stick out your tongue (see STICKING OUT OF THE TONGUE, page 128).**

Variations of Performance: You may use two hands in tandem to make the nose even longer (and the taunt even greater). Additionally, the splayed fingers may be wiggled or held still, depending on preference.

63. **UP YOURS**

Usage and Origins:	*The forearm of one arm jerks upward as the fist or palm of the opposite hand slaps down hard at its elbow.* The up yours gesture is generally meant as a sexual insult, and it literally translates to "Up your anus." It is meant to mime the action of a penis becoming erect, and it is most often used as a phallic threat from one man to another.

This gesture, which often goes by the euphemistic name "forearm jerk," may be used in Britain to indicate that a woman is so sexually attractive that a man is getting an erection at that moment, but it is performed to elicit the disrespectful, obscenely insulting interpretation everywhere else.

Region: The up yours gesture is employed as an insult throughout the Americas and Europe, as well as in several other countries, whose variations are listed on the following page (see "Variations of Performance"). Avoid the use of this gesture in Malta, where it is illegal.

Environment: Because men lose their tempers in an endless variety of locales, it is difficult to pinpoint specific spots where an increased use of the up yours gesture will occur. Certainly bars, sporting events, and parking lots will see heightened usage due to frustration and/or inebriation.

Execution:

1. Hold both arms straight out so they are perpendicular to your body, palms up.

2. Make both hands into fists, with your palms facing up. Or make the right hand into a fist and leave the left hand flat.

3. Put your left fist or palm in the crook of your right elbow [FIG. A].

4. Quickly bend your right arm, raising your right fist until your forearm is pressing against your left hand.

FIG. A

Variations of Performance:

The variations of this gesture do not change its basic meaning, only the intensity of the insult. In Italy, the forearm jerks forward instead of upward, imitating actual penetration rather than just an erection. In Lebanon and Syria, to gesture "up yours," a person thrusts his right fist through his loosely curled left hand; here the fist is the penis being thrust into an orifice, the curled hand.

In Yugoslavia, only one arm is used to employ this gesture—the arm with the fisted hand is jerked upward.

In Brazil, the middle finger of the hand that is jerked upward is raised; this is known as the "banana."

64.   **"V" ON THE NOSE**

Usage and Origins:

The index and middle fingers splay out to make a "V," which is then placed at the base of the nose. Like most obscene gestures, the "V" on the nose gesture mimes sexual intercourse, with the fingers standing for the vagina and the nose symbolizing the penis. Also like most obscene gestures, this one is used as an insult. It is used in much the same way the middle finger gesture is used; that is, to indicate rage or disrespect (see page 117).

Region:

This gesture is common in parts of Central and South America, as well as the Middle East.

Environment: Anger and derision are expressed in a variety of locales, so the "V" on the nose gesture will be seen everywhere from neighborhood bars to gridlocked traffic.

Execution: 1.   Make a fist.

2.   Extend your index and middle fingers to form a "V."

3.   Raise your arm and place the crotch of the "V" against the base of your nose.

VI. Just for Emphasis

65. 📷 **BUSTY**

Usage and Origins:

The hands are cupped and pumped once near the chest, as if they are grabbing a pair of breasts. This gesture is used to indicate that a woman is particularly voluptuous. The one who performs the gesture clearly appreciates this in some way, though this does not make it a polite signal. It is rather rude, is largely employed by men, and may be evoked after a woman passes by in order to let companions know you approved of her figure.

The busty gesture may also be directed at a buxom woman to let her know you enjoy looking at her breasts, though this is even more impolite.

Finally, this gesture is often used to indicate a woman who is not present, in order to make it clear about whom you are talking, as in, "You know, Mary. She's the one . . ." and the gesture is performed, as though cup size is Mary's only defining characteristic.

Region:

Due to the obviousness of the meaning of this gesture, it will be widely understood, even in areas where it may not ever have been used before. It is not recommended that this gesture be bandied about wildly, however, as some Muslim nations' laws regarding physical commentary on women, as well as the way women ought to be addressed, are strict, and transgressions are often punishable by jail.

Environment: Men are more likely to employ this gesture while in groups, so places where men may congregate and women may pass are good spots to see this gesture in its habitat. Some of these are bars, street corners, construction sites, or sporting events, though this is in no way an exhaustive list, as buxom women and groups of men cross paths just about everywhere.

Execution:

1. **With fingers open and palms facing your body, bring both hands up to chest level.**

2. **Cup hands slightly.**

3. **Pump both hands toward the body a few times [FIG. A].**

FIG. A

Variations of
Performance:

In Greece, men will thump their chests using both hands to symbolize female breasts.

66. **CHIN STROKE**

Usage and
Origins:

The thumb and forefinger scrape the sides of the chin.
The chin stroke is generally believed to come from the act of stroking a beard, or at least the place where a beard would grow. It is often used unconsciously when an individual is deep in thought. Oddly, it is used more among clean-shaven men than hirsute ones. The chin stroke is also used pointedly, as in, "Let me think that over for a moment."

In Saudi Arabia, this gesture is a conscious one and is performed as a sign of great respect. The action is meant to imply a beard, which is a symbol of maturity and the wisdom that comes with it.

In France, Italy, Holland, and Germany, this gesture is used in much the same insulting way as the chin flick gesture (see page 107). Here it is employed to let another know that his story is so long that you will have a full beard by the time he has finished telling it. In other words, the speaker is boring and should stop talking as soon as possible.

Region:

This gesture is used worldwide; see "Usage and Origins" for how it will be understood across cultures.

Environment: Individuals may find themselves deep in thought in any
                number of locales, from the library to the laboratory.

Execution: 1. Tilt your head back and to one side slightly.

                2. Reach for your chin with one hand.

                3. Cup your hand around your chin, thumb to one
                   side and fingers to the other.

                4. Softly stroke the sides of the chin with your
                   fingertips.

                5. The entire length of the fingers is brought into
                   play, but the contact is primarily between the
                   fingertips and the chin.

Variations of   In Brazil, a conscious variation of this gesture is used
Performance: when a deal has been sealed. The thumb and index
                finger stroke the chin, but just under the lips instead
                of along the jaw line.

67.   **CROSS MY HEART**

Usage and   *The index finger of one hand traces an "X" over the left*
Origins: *breast, in the general location of the heart.* Predictably,
                the cross my heart gesture has its roots as a Christian

religious gesture to indicate the crucifix. Historians believe that before the fourth century A.D., it was performed with the thumb and index finger on the forehead.

Dating from the fourth century on, the heart was crossed as well, and by the tenth century, the heart cross had grown into a full cross of the upper body. (This cross is still used today as the Catholic sign of blessing oneself.)

The cross my heart gesture is now used as a secular oath and is often accompanied by "Cross my heart and hope to die" to indicate that this promise will not be broken. The religious meaning still survives in some circles but has largely fallen away, though the gesture is primarily seen only in Christian countries.

Region: You will rarely see this gesture outside of predominately Christian countries.

Environment: Promises are made in a variety of places, so this gesture will be seen everywhere from restaurants to backyards to bowling alleys. In elementary schools, children often perform this gesture to verify a statement, accompanied by the rhyme: "Cross my heart and hope to die / stick a needle in my eye."

The full upper-body cross will most often be seen in churches, though you may witness pious Catholics crossing themselves in any number of locales.

Execution: 1. Make a loose fist with one hand [FIG. A].

2. Extend your index finger [FIG. B].

3. Raise your finger to the left side of your chest.

4. Trace an "X" over your heart [FIG. C].

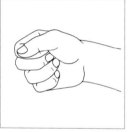

FIG. A

FIG. B

FIG. C

Variations of
Performance:

The full upper-body cross that is performed as the Catholic blessing is done with the index finger extended or simply the whole hand, beginning at the forehead and continuing down to the chest, then from left shoulder to right shoulder.

68. **EYELID PULL**

Usage and
Origins:

The index finger pulls the eyelid of one eye down. In most cultures, the main idea behind this gesture is alertness, whether it is indicative of the gesturer or the one being gestured to. It may mean that the gesturer has figured something out or is gesturing to another to keep their eyes open and be cautious.

The eyelid pull gesture may also refer to the fact that you are not fooled by another's trickery. It will be used to indicate awareness of being made fun of or that something suspicious is going on.

Region:

While this gesture is uncommon in North America, its meaning is fairly obvious and will be understood most anywhere. The eyelid pull gesture is used in most European countries to mean both an awareness of a thing and a plea to be aware.

In South America, the eyelid pull gesture is often performed to indicate that a woman is attractive, or a real "eyeful."

Finally, in Yugoslavia, it may be invoked to refer to disappointment or sadness, as if pointing to a tear.

Environment: The occasions for attentiveness are many and varied. The lookout in any kind of illegal activity will often be flashed the eyelid pull gesture outside of a bank, jewelry shop, or convenience store, but illegal activities are not the only ones that require participants to be on the alert.

Sporting matches, kitchens, and taxi stands are all spots where vigilance is necessary, and these areas may see an increased usage of the eyelid pull gesture.

Execution: 1. **Make a fist** [Fig. A].

2. **Extend your index finger** [Fig. B].

3. **Use the index finger to pull down the bottom corner of one eye.**

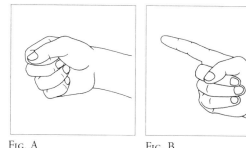

Fig. A   Fig. B

69. 📷 **FINGER DRUM**

Usage and Origins:

The fingertips of one hand strike a surface in quick succession, repeatedly. The finger drum gesture is one that evolved from the unconscious action that often occurs when a person wants to escape or run away, or when he has lost patience while waiting for someone or some event. Experts posit that in this case, our hands show that what we really want is to get up and leave or get things moving.

This gesture has survived the evolution of our species; it is a vestige from our days as primates when we walked on all fours and our hands were involved in our movement. As a gesture of impatience or anxiety, the finger drum gesture is practiced, either intentionally or unintentionally, to show the frustration that comes with these feelings and is often accompanied by deep sighs.

Region:

Since drumming the fingers originated from a reflexive bit of body language, it will be used and understood worldwide.

Environment:

When finger-drumming occurs as a reflex, it will be seen just about anywhere. Particular spots to see anxious and impatient people drumming their fingers purposeful are hospital and doctor's waiting rooms, college campuses around exam time, and in train

stations or airports, especially when an arrival has
been delayed.

Execution: 1.   Rest one of your hands on a surface, with the
                  heel of your hand and the tips of your fingers
                  making contact with the surface.

             2.   Tap the tip of each finger on the surface in turn.

             3.   Repeat the tapping slowly or quickly, depending
                  on the level of boredom or frustration.

70.   **FINGER SNAP**

Usage and   *The thumb and middle finger are rubbed together*
Origins: *quickly to make a clicking noise.* Finger-snapping has
              its roots in ancient Rome, where it was employed to
              gain the attention of idle servants at the table.

              These days, it has a number of functions but is
              generally still used to get another person's attention or
              to tell her that you are impatient, and she should
              hurry up. In many areas, this form of attention-getting
              is considered rude and self-centered, though there are
              some cultures where it is still customary to call servants
              in this way.

              Often, you will see a person snapping his fingers
              while trying to remember a word or name, or doing

so just as he remembers what he was puzzling over.

When using the finger snap gesture to keep time with music, there is no hidden meaning; the fingers simply act as a metronome or another instrument.

Region: The various meanings for this gesture will be understood throughout the Western world and in the Middle East.

Environment: Restaurants and opulent dining rooms that contain servants are spots where this gesture will be used, regardless of its appropriateness.

Any place where people puzzle over an answer to or meaning of some question—from examination rooms to game-show sets—will be areas to see this gesture in use as an audible nudge toward recognition.

Concerts and musical events of all kinds will see countless people keeping time with the finger snap gesture.

Execution: 1. **Hold your thumb tightly against the middle finger.**

2. **While pressing the fingertips together, slide the thumb up and the finger down.**

3. **Do it quickly, and a sharp snapping sound should be audible.**

Variations of Performance:	In France and some Latin American countries, snapping the fingers of both hands at once may carry obscene undertones.

71. **FINGERNAIL BUFF**

Usage and Origins:	*The fingernails of one hand are brushed against the chest, as if to polish them.* The fingernail buff conveys a feeling of lighthearted self-praise, and is often performed after you've said something particularly clever, whether in an argument or in simple conversation. This is a gesture that will often be employed at parties or other social events when one tells a story that involves a bit of harmless bragging, such as a tale of getting a date or receiving a promotion.
Region:	The fingernail buff is common in Europe and the Americas.
Environment:	Parties, informal gatherings, or any other social events where one person is seen telling others a story in which he fares particularly well are spots to see the fingernail buff gesture in action.

Execution: 1. **Curl your fingers down so that they align with the top of the palm.**

2. **Raise your arm until your hand reaches your chest easily.**

3. **Lightly brush your fingertips against your upper chest, moving up and down two times [FIG. A].**

FIG. A

Variations of Performance: Some people will exhale lightly on their fingernails prior to buffing them [FIG. B]. This is similar to people who exhale on their spectacles before cleaning the lenses.

Fig. B

72. **THE FIST**

Usage and
Origins:

The fist is raised above the head. The raised fist is a gesture of unity, defiance, and sometimes triumph. The gesture became a trademark of the Black Power movement of the 1960s and was used very publicly by Martin Luther King, Jr., throughout many protest marches.

At the 1968 Olympics in Mexico, when American sprinters Tommie Smith and John Carlos ascended to accept their medals, they bowed their heads and raised their black-gloved fists, shocking the nation and the Olympics Committee—the runners were suspended and kicked out of the Olympic Village.

These days, the fist gesture is often used in a celebratory manner by athletes, politicians, and audiences and may be pumped or remain stationary. When the fist is pumped in the air, the number of pumps will indicate the level of excitement being expressed.

Region: The fist gesture is used throughout the world.

Environment: Apart from the famous Black Power examples above, there are myriad places to see the fist in action. During his tour of the United States and Europe in 1990, Nelson Mandela often employed the stationary fist as a gesture of unity and empowerment.

Audiences in sporting arenas, concert venues, and live comedy forums are often seen pumping their fists in celebration and agreement; one spot where this was prevalent was on *The Arsenio Hall Show* of the late 1980s.

Anywhere excitement mounts is a chance to see the fist gesture in any of its incarnations.

Execution: 1. **Curl all the fingers of one hand tight against the palm** [Fig. A].

2. **Hold your thumb tightly against the side of the fist.**

3. Orient your fist so the palm faces out.

4. Raise your arm straight above your head.

Fig. A

Variations of Performance:

To make an angry, threatening gesture, turn the fist around as though about to punch someone, with the knuckles facing out. You may also incorporate shaking the fist into this gesture, though this is rarely done outside of cartoons or old movies with stereotypically exaggerated villains.

The fist may also be pumped in the air beside the head in order to express extreme excitement or approval.

73. 📷 **HAND CHOP**

Usage and
Origins:

One hand is held flat and stiff, slashing the air and occasionally hitting the upturned palm of the other hand. The hand chop gesture is often manifested as an unconscious bit of body language, occurring largely among people who tend to gesticulate with their hands while talking. This gesture is used to illustrate a specific point in an argument or to elicit a break-through in a confusing conversation in order to make a definitive point.

It is used intentionally in much the same ways, to add a forceful note to an order or punctuate a dynamic point in a speech. The hand chop gesture symbolically hacks through any secondary information in order to get to the crux of a situation and will be used both as an involuntary signal and a deliberate one in this way.

Region:

Since the hand chop originated from a reflexive bit of body language, the gesture is used worldwide.

Environment:

Any area in which important discussions are held and points are made will see use of the hand chop gesture. This means that you'll encounter the gesture in conference rooms, debate auditoriums, university halls, and any locale that is frequented by those who enjoy arguing.

Execution: 1. **Make a paddle with one hand.**

2. **As you speak, raise your arm at the elbow.**

3. **Drop your arm, slashing the air [FIG. A].**

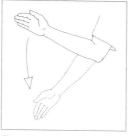

FIG. A

Variations of   The hand can also be dropped into the opposite hand.
Performance: This lends an audible component to the gesture's performance, further emphasizing your point.

In Italy, if the hand is chopped through the air
without the use of the second hand, it is taken as a
threat, meaning that if another person doesn't immediately stop whatever he is doing, the gesturer might
haul off and hit him. This variation is often practiced
by exasperated parents toward misbehaving children.

74. 📷 **HAND PURSE**

Usage and Origins:

The tips of all four fingers and thumb come together at a point and are shaken as one. Like many gestures that are hand-centered, the hand purse began as what anthropologists call a "baton" gesture, or one that is performed almost unconsciously when speaking. This is done to help illustrate speech by emphasizing the rhythm of the words. The hand purse gesture is most often employed unknowingly to advance a fine point in an argument. Since many speakers, public or other-wise, use their hands often while speaking, a more conscious form of the gesture has developed and helps an argument along in much the same way as the unconscious version.

This geture is commonly seen throughout the world, but most often in Italy and areas of the United States where there are large communities of Italian-Americans, such as New York City and parts of New Jersey and Pennsylvania. In this case, the hand purse gesture is generally used as a query for precise infor-mation, essentially translating to "Explain exactly what you mean." It may be more strident, as in, "What do you want?" and will indicate that the gesturer is becoming frustrated with the speaker. Sometimes, it will become even more snappish, meaning "You fool!"

The intent can be fully determined by the force with which the fingers are pressed together or the furiousness of the shaking motion.

Region: The hand purse gesture is seen worldwide as an unconscious gesture, though it is most common in Italy. There are a variety of different regional variations and meanings assigned to this gesture, listed below in "Variations of Performance."

Environment: Since people often need clarification and become frustrated when they don't get it, there will be few places that won't see the deliberate use of the hand purse gesture come into play. It will be seen everywhere from the farmer's market to the firemen's ball. This is also true of the unconscious version.

Execution: 1. **Raise your hand to chest level in front of your body.**

2. **Press the tips of your fingers to your thumb.**

3. **Shake your hand back and forth or up and down.**

Variations of Performance: In Greece and Turkey, if the pursed hand makes one downward movement it means "good" and is similar to the continental fingertip kiss (see BLOWN KISS, page 2), but with without a kiss being mimed. In Malta, this same gesture can be meant sarcastically, to indicate that something is bad by calling it good. For example, you might employ this at a sporting event when a team is performing badly.

In Belgium, France, and Portugal, forming this gesture, then opening and closing the fingertips slightly, indicates fear, as when the sphincter muscles open and close quickly in a moment of panic.

In Yugoslavia, Spain, the Canary Islands, and the Spanish-speaking nations of South America, when the fingers open and close just a little bit several times, it refers to a large number of people in a crowd.

In the Arab cultures of northern Africa and the Middle East and in Tunisia, if the hand moves slowly upward, the meaning translates to "Slow down" or "Be patient." This gesture is often used on the road to indicate concern to another driver.

Finally, if the hand is pursed and then turned on its side and brought to the mouth, as if it is holding food, it is understood as a basic miming action that shows hunger and is understood the world over.

75. **HAND RUB**

Usage and Origins:
Both hands are rubbed together, palm touching palm. The hand rub is a gesture that originated as a natural reaction to cold weather—the friction caused by rubbing the hands together warms them up. This gesture is still employed in order to convey that a chill in the

air is making one uncomfortable, whether it is unintentional or deliberate.

Another way to understand the hand rub gesture is as an anticipatory gesture; a person may rub his hands together when he is about to receive a gift, or just before a delicious platter of food is set before him in anticipation of having it in his hands, so to speak.

This expectant form is also seen when someone— a diabolical genius or even an evil person of average intelligence—is plotting against someone or something and is eagerly awaiting downfall and destruction.

Region:

The hand rub gesture is widespread but is possibly more common in colder Northern countries than in those near the equator.

In South America, this gesture is used to show that two women are lesbians.

Environment:

Campsites in winter are a good time to see outdoorsy folk rubbing their hands together, in front of the campfire or otherwise. Ski lodges, the Winter Olympics, and other snow-covered sites will be chilly—winter-sports enthusiasts will demonstrate this fact with their hands even when wearing gloves.

When used in excited anxiousness, this gesture may be seen most anywhere, from the dining room to the bedroom and from birthday parties to banquet halls.

Execution: 1. **Flatten both hands.**

2. **Raise them to chest level at a comfortable distance from your body.**

3. **Bring them together, palm touching palm.**

4. **Swiftly rub them back and forth over one another.**

Variations of   In Saudi Arabia, if the hands are rubbed together with
Performance: the fingers slightly curled and grasping the other hand,
it is construed as a symbol of grief and regret that
translates to "wringing hands in grief."

---

76.   **THE HORNS**

Usage and   *The index and pinkie fingers are extended from a fist;*
Origins: *the gesture resembles a horned animal.* Due to the fact
that this gesture is more than 2,500 years old, its origin is lost, but its primary usage now and throughout
history is to indicate that someone's wife is cheating on
him. Historians have many theories about the origin
of this meaning; it is largely thought to be representative of a bull, an animal that is generally castrated to
prevent violence. To flash the horns gesture at a cuckold is to say, "Look at what a bull you are—your wife
has to cheat on you to be satisfied." It may also mean

"Your wife has castrated you by having an affair."

There is another way to perform the horns gesture that carries with it a lesser-known, secondary meaning: If the fingers are pointed away instead of up, the gesture takes on a meaning of protection from evil or bad luck associated with the Evil Eye.

Before Christianity, ancient people used the symbol to call on the great horned bull, a protective god. As Christianity gained momentum, this horned god grew to be thought of as the devil, so those who still practiced this gesture as a protective measure were actually calling on the devil to ward away evil or bad luck. Lucky charms depicting this version of the gesture are still sold in Mediterranean countries, including Italy.

In the late twentieth century, heavy-metal singer Ronny James Dio of the band Black Sabbath popularized this gesture among fans of hard rock. He learned the gesture from his Italian grandmother, who invoked it to ward off the Evil Eye. He performed the protective horns gesture incorrectly, however: Instead of pointing away to ward off evil, the horns pointed up to accuse adultery.

Incorrect or not, soon the gesture took hold as a trademark symbol of heavy-metal music and was waved effusively at concerts from Judas Priest to Megadeth— the extremely old gesture was given new life as a not-so-secret handshake. In the 1990s, the horns became an ironic gesture used to make fun of them and their choice of music.

Region: In southern Europe and near the Mediterranean, especially in Spain, Portugal, Italy, and Malta, the horns are used primarily to mean that a wife is cheating on a husband. In Italy and Malta, the gesture also hangs on as a symbol to keep away evil and bad luck.

As a rock 'n' roll symbol, its use will be seen in the United States, the United Kingdom, and other countries where hard rock made its indelible mark.

A small, regional alternative meaning can be found in Texas, where this gesture is symbolic of the Longhorns of the University of Texas.

Environment: The horns gesture will be seen in a variety of venues to let a man know his wife has been unfaithful; perhaps other men, on a night out at the local pub, will let their buddy know of his mate's adultery, or perhaps they will use the horns gesture as an insult across the bar in response to men they don't like.

As a protection against evil, this gesture will be used anywhere from dark alleys to an enemy's neighborhood. You will witness the horns as a rock symbol in venues both large and small as fans are caught up in the excitement of the music.

Finally, in Texas, you will see the horns performed in the stadiums of the university system, as well as anywhere Longhorn fans congregate.

Execution: 1. **Make a fist with one hand.**

2. **Extend your index and pinkie fingers.**

3. **Raise your hand and point the fingers up or away from your body, depending on meaning.**

Variations of
Performance: In South America, this gesture, when performed with a rotation at the wrist, has a similar meaning to the protective gesture in Italy and Malta, but it comes from a different source. It is known as the lizard gesture (*lagarto*) and is a superstitious counteraction to someone who has said the taboo word *culebra*, or "snake."

77. **MONEY**

Usage and
Origins: *The thumb and fingertips of the same hand rub one another.* The money gesture mimes the action of rubbing a coin in one's fingers and is commonly used when talking about money. The context for this gesture varies significantly: It may indicate a request for payment, let someone know that something is too expensive (as in "It'll cost you!"), or request charity from a stranger.

The money gesture may also be used to tacitly ask

another about a delicate financial issue, perhaps concerning salary, where not saying the word makes the question seem less crass. Similarly, when discussing money that is used for or attained through illegal means, use of this gesture helps keep unsavory matters hush-hush.

An unrelated and generally unconsciously used meaning of this gesture involves the texture of a thing; it will be used to ask how something felt or to indicate that it felt soft or rough.

Region:
The money gesture is used all over the world to refer to any number of financial matters, as well as to discuss texture.

Environment:
Since it is popularly believed that, by turns, money makes the world go 'round, money buys happiness, or money changes everything, it will be impossible to escape the use of this gesture in any locale. Homes, offices, street corners, alleyways, boutiques, restaurants—all will see talk of money.

When used as a way to discreetly inquire about a financial issue, the money gesture will be seen most often at office functions where liquor is served and coworkers become less shy about asking improper questions.

Execution:

1. Bring the tips of your fingers against the tip of your thumb.

2. Move the fingers and the thumb in opposite directions, rubbing against each other lightly.

3. Repeat several times.

4. To emphasize the amount of money being discussed, exhale slowly, whistling softly.

Variations of Performance:

Holding a palm out flat or cupping the hands is also used as a gesture to request money.

78. **NOSE TAP**

Usage and Origins:

The side of the nose is tapped with the tip of the index finger. The nose tap gesture is done to imply collusion between two individuals, as if to say, "You and I have a secret that we won't tell anyone else, though others will try to sniff it out." The idea of metaphorically sniffing out wrongdoing comes from criminals, called "nosers," who were paid by the police to inform on other criminals. If one perpetrator tapped his nose at another, it meant that they should be silent, as there was a noser around.

In a related meaning that doesn't imply complicity

between gesturers, the tap on the nose conveys that someone is nosing around where he shouldn't be and that those around should keep their mouths shut.

Another extension of this is a threat; you may tap your nose to indicate that you have ascertained what another is up to, and you will cause trouble if he doesn't cease and desist in this activity.

This gesture may also imply nosiness, and from there, it has evolved into another interpretation: The nose tap gesture can be used to indicate that someone has figured out a secret, as in, "You guessed it right on the nose." In this case, the tip of the nose is tapped.

Region: All of the above meanings are common in North America, as well as in the British Isles and Italian-speaking regions.

Environment: Areas where criminals get together to plan heists, such as basements, alleys, and bars, will see a fair amount of this gesture. Police stations, the back of the paddy wagon, and prison might also be places to witness this gesture in use.

It is also used to mean "You got it!" in games of charades, right in your living room or den.

Execution: 1. **Make a fist with one hand** [Fig. A].

2. **Extend your index finger** [Fig. B].

3. **Raise your hand and touch the side of the nose with the tip of your finger.**

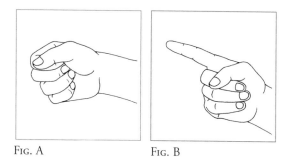

Fig. A   Fig. B

Variations of Performance:

Lightly touching the tip of your nose, as opposed to the side, can mean "right on." This gesture may also be used in Libya, Saudi Arabia, and Syria to convey that a solemn commitment has been made.

79. **ONE**

Usage and Origins:

The hand is held in a fist, with the index finger extended and pointing upward. The one gesture is a multi-faceted gesture that, in the United States and other countries where the index finger represents the number one, is often flashed to say "Just one second" or "I'll be with you in one moment." This lets the person who requires attention know that you will help her as soon as you have finished what you're currently busy with.

Similarly, this gesture may be used by the person who is requesting help or service; in this context it means "Excuse me" or "I need one moment of your time" and is a polite and unobtrusive way to get the attention of a store clerk, waiter, or teacher without undue interference.

Since the index finger often stands for number one in Western countries, it may also be extended in order to say "I'm number one" or "Our team or candidate is number one."

Region: This gesture will be used in both of the ways described above in most Western countries, where the extended index finger means "one."

Environment: Anywhere service or information may be required from a busy individual—such as a classroom, a restaurant, a visitors' center, or any type of store—is a location to see the one gesture used by questioners and answerers alike.

To indicate that you, someone else, or a group that you support is number one in your book, you might use this gesture at a sporting event or political rally.

Execution: 1. Make a fist with one hand [Fig. A].

2. Extend your index finger [Fig. B].

3. Bring your hand to shoulder level at a comfortable distance from your body.

4. Turn your hand so that the palm is facing out.

5. Move your hand slightly for emphasis.

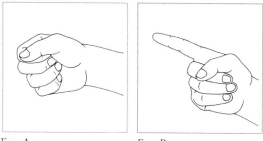

Fig. A   Fig. B

Variations of   If the palm faces sideways instead of straight out, and
Performance: is shaken rather than still, the index finger may be
used to represent a small club being waved threaten-
ingly at another to mean that he should pay attention.
This is seen all over the world. This gesture should
not be confused with THE POINT (see page 170).

80. 📷   **THE POINT**

Usage and   *The hand is held in a fist, with the index finger extended*
Origins: *and directed toward someone or something.* The primary
meaning of the point gesture is to show direction, or
to refer to something that may or may not be close
enough to touch. This is an inherent gesture in humans
that in some cultures must be unlearned due to rules
of etiquette.

In many Western countries, it is considered impolite to point at other individuals, and therefore other
ways of indicating the person about whom you are
speaking must be found. Parents the world over teach
their children that it is not nice to point, though you
will still see this gesture in use.

The point gesture can also be considered a threat
when used during heated conversation or confronta-
tion. In this case, the point gesture is used as a symbolic weapon that can be used to stab one's adversary.
It is from this adversarial meaning that the point
gesture attained its status as an impolite gesture.

Region: Both meanings above are understood around the
world, but can be impolite in many cultures.

Environment: Crowded areas, such as large parties, concerts, or lectures can often make pointing a necessity to avoid
confusion about who is being referred to. Candy

shops, pharmacies, and other retail areas where products are out of reach of consumers will see a fair amount of pointing to indicate what goods are required. Heated debate arises in various locales, though conference rooms, pubs, and forensic team competitions will see heightened occurrence of the point.

Execution: 1. **Make a fist** [FIG. A].

2. **Extend your index finger** [FIG. B].

3. **Aim your index finger at something.**

4. **Feel free to move your arm around as necessary to make it clear what you are referring to.**

FIG. A   FIG. B

Variations of Performance:	In Central and South America, the head point is common; a tilt of the head accomplishes the same goal as the finger point gesture, but is less rude. As a variation of this, Native Americans generally point with their lips or chins.
	In Japan and China, pointing is done with the whole hand, and Malaysians point with their thumbs.

81.   **SCRATCHING OF THE HEAD**

Usage and Origins:	*The fingers of one hand scratch the head.* Head-scratching is a natural gesture employed by humans when they are puzzled. Like many unconscious gestures, the scratching of the head gesture may be accentuated and stylized and then performed deliberately in order to illustrate confusion or bemusement. This gesture may also be used when an individual is trying to solve a particularly difficult problem.
Region:	Like all gestures that originate from natural reflexes, this gesture will be seen the world over.
Environment:	The scratching of the head gesture will be seen virtually everywhere one is confronted with implausible or incomprehensible situations, from the TV room when the evening news is on to the highway when another motorist appears lost.

Academic classes such as philosophy, calculus, or physics may elicit both unconscious and deliberate head-scratching, especially in an examination room or lecture hall. Cinema-goers may find themselves scratching their heads during obtuse foreign films.

Execution:

1. **Raise one hand to the top of your head.**

2. **Scratch your head lightly with one finger.**

3. **Furrow your brow.**

4. **Squint your eyes.**

5. **Drop your arm.**

Variations of Performance:

You may use one or all of your fingers—or any number in between—to accomplish the scratching of the head.

82. **SHHH!**

Usage and Origins:

The index finger is held in front of the lips, while a quiet "shhh" sound is vocalized. This gesture works in two parts: The finger in front of the lips blocks the source of sound, while the "shhh!" sound quiets the person on the receiving end of the gesture.

There are two possibilities for why this is the sound used to accompany this gesture: It may be because it is the first sound of the word "shut," implying that another should shut his mouth and no longer speak or make noise. Since the shhh! gesture may also be gentle, another possible origin for the accompanying sound could be from childhood, when mothers quiet and comfort children with the gentle noise.

The level of insistence or comfort of the shhh! gesture is conveyed through facial expression and the speed at which the gesture is performed.

Region: This gesture is used all over the world to indicate the need for quiet.

Environment: The library, where it behooves one to ask for silence quietly, is perhaps the single most common spot to experience the use of the shhh! gesture. Similarly, movie theaters, train compartments, testing rooms, and near a baby's bassinet are likely locales to see the shhh! gesture in action.

Execution: 1. **Purse your lips.**

2. **Make a fist with one hand** [Fig. A].

3. **Extend the index finger** [Fig. B].

4. Place the outside edge of the extended index finger against your lips.

5. This gesture may be punctuated with the actual sound "Shhh!"

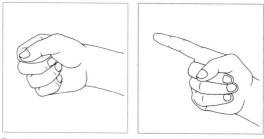

Fig. A   Fig. B

Variations of Performance:
In Saudi Arabia, one simply brings the finger to the lips and blows on the finger instead of making the "shhh" sound in order to attain silence.

83. **SHOCKING!**

Usage and Origins:
One hand covers the open mouth. The shocking! gesture may be used by the gesturer to keep his own words—whether they be false or inappropriate—from escaping his mouth. Alternatively, a person may cover his

mouth in reaction to another's words or actions, whether unbelievable, amazing, or simply not true.

This is a gesture whose spirit can be serious, in which case it will most likely be innate or reflex-based, or it may be done sarcastically, in which case it is deliberate. When done pointedly, the shocking! gesture is more an exaggeration of shock or dismay to untruths spoken by the gesturer or another party.

In some cases, the hand covers the mouth as a natural reaction to a person's uncomfortable feelings about lying. Since this gives away the fact that one is lying, it is one of the first and easiest reflexes for a serial liar to phase out of his body language repertoire.

Region:

This gesture is used across the world but is most common in Europe and the Americas.

Environment:

Unbelievable things and fabrication seem to happen regardless of place. Bars, taverns, social gatherings, and other places where liquor is abundant will see increased usage of this gesture, as alcohol has a tendency to exponentially multiply the amount of embellishment that is natural when relating a story.

Execution:

1. **Drop your jaw, opening your mouth wide and in the shape of an "O."**

2. **Flatten one hand, pressing the fingers together.**

3. Raise the hand toward your mouth, with your palm facing you.

4. Cover your mouth with your fingers.

Variations of Performance:
You may or may not actually make contact with your mouth, depending on how quickly you perform the gesture. To accentuate shock, you may raise your eyebrows and widen your eyes while performing the standard shocking! gesture.

84.   **THE SHRUG**

Usage and Origins:
The shoulders and eyebrows are briefly raised, while at the same time, the lower lip curls down and the palms are rotated up. The shrug gesture is generally used to mean "I don't know" or to indicate indifference to a question that calls for a decision. Experts believe that this gesture originated as one of defensiveness: The person shrugging feels vulnerable and takes a posture of trying to appear larger by raising the shoulders and moving the hands.

This vulnerability arises because he feels helpless for being without an answer or any helpful advice or solution. This meaning is less present in a shrug that is offered by a sullen teenager when he is asked what he wants for dinner; in this instance and similar ones, the shrug gesture indicates such supreme apathy as to suggest that the questioner, usually a parent, is woefully stupid for even asking.

Region: Though this gesture is in use worldwide, it is less common in Asian cultures.

Environment: Since people often find better ways to communicate doubt, indifference, and indecision as they get older, you will mainly see the shrug gesture used among children and teenagers, especially in elementary and middle schools.

However, since the shrug is such a basic gesture that conveys so much, and because doubt and a lack of knowledge are pervasive in the world, this gesture will be performed virtually anywhere, from restaurants and railroad stations to boutiques and ballgames.

Execution: 1. **Let your arms hang fully extended at your sides.**

2. **Incline your head forward slightly.**

3. **Raise your forearms at the elbow until your hands are at chest level, with palms open and facing upward.**

4. **Simultaneously raise your shoulders to your ears.**

5. Simultaneously jut your chin down slightly, raise your eyebrows, and curl out your lower lip.

6. Return to your resting position.

Variations of Performance:

It is common to perform only one or two pieces of this multipart gesture to express the same sentiments. You may use your shoulders alone, or even just one shoulder; you may rotate your palms upward, or even just one; you may lower the corners of your mouth; or you may just raise the eyebrows quickly. Each of these, as well as any combination of them, will convey that you just don't know.

85.   **SO-SO**

Usage and Origins:

The hand is held open and tilted from left to right. The so-so gesture is a gesture whose origins are unknown. The rocking of the hand seems to suggest vacillation on the part of the gesturer, and the gesture's meaning reflects this. Somewhere between a THUMBS-UP and a THUMBS-DOWN (see page 52), this signal should be taken to mean ambivalence and a non-committal attitude.

You will often see this gesture used as a response to the question, "How are you?" The person for whom the gesture is performed will be expected to inquire as to what may be wrong, as the so-so gesture is rarely used without a desire to elaborate in words. When used in response to the question "How was it?" this gesture says it all: It wasn't great, but it wasn't dreadful, either.

Whether referring to a movie, a date, or a dinner, the so-so gesture is a very descriptive and telling gesture.

Region: This gesture will be used and understood largely in Western cultures.

Environment: Restaurants, theaters, bookstores, and malls are all places where opinions on products are asked and answered, but the so-so gesture won't be limited to these locations. Any locale where a rating is required will see this gesture in use.

Execution: 1. Make a flat paddle with one hand.

2. Extend your hand palm down, mid torso. (Do not hold your hand out at arm's length; a bent elbow is fine.)

3. Tilt your hand down to the right.

4. Return the hand to its neutral position.

5. Tilt your hand down to the left.

6. **Repeat.**

7. **Frown slightly.**

86. **UP TO HERE**

Usage and Origins:

The forehead is tapped by the palm, which is held face down. The up to here gesture originated as a gesture to indicate that one was full of food and could not eat any more. From here, it evolved to mean that a person was exasperated to the point of not being able to deal any further with whatever it was that was irritating or emotionally taxing—this is the meaning behind the gesture's modern use. It is often accompanied by the phrase, "I've had it up to here."

Mothers and fathers are particularly fond of this gesture and its coinciding statement, and it is often followed by a gentle—or perhaps not so gentle— threat, as in, "Clean your room or you're grounded for a month!" Teachers will also use this gesture fairly often, especially when students are particularly rambunctious, as before a holiday.

Though its performance resembles the salute gesture (see page 27), its meaning is very different, and context will certainly indicate which meaning is meant.

Region: The up to here gesture is commonly used in Western Europe and the Americas.

Environment: Recalcitrant children's bedrooms will be a good spot to see this gesture enjoy increased usage, as will elementary and middle school classrooms and day care facilities. The up to here gesture will not be confined to these areas, however, as exasperation rears its ugly head most anywhere, from the office to the garage.

Execution:
1. **Flatten one hand, pressing the fingers together.**

2. **With your palm facing down, raise your hand to touch your forehead, just above your eyebrows.**

3. **Tap your forehead several times.**

Variations of Performance: Instead of the forehead, the chin may be tapped to indicate frustration. In South America, the up to here gesture is performed with a tap to the top of the head.

87. **YADDA YADDA YADDA**

Usage and Origins: *The hand is splayed and moved in a circle to move conversation along.* The yadda yadda yadda gesture, or at least the name given to indicate it, was popularized in the 1990s in the United States after a much talked-about episode of the sitcom *Seinfeld*. The characters used this gesture as a sort of verbal ellipsis to skip over the details of tales they were relating.

It is clear from context that the yadda yadda yadda gesture is used to move the conversation along by skipping over something that is not particularly relevant to the speaker, and this is the way the gesture has been used since the airing of the episode.

In anthropological terms, this is a "baton" gesture, or a gesture that, like many others in this chapter (see HAND PURSE, page 155), is performed almost unconsciously by the hands when one is speaking to help illustrate a point by emphasizing the rhythm of the words.

Region:

Though the yadda yadda yadda gesture is used less today than it was in the mid-1990s when *Seinfeld* was in its heyday, you will still see the occasional use in Western cultures, especially the United States.

Environment:

Bars, diners, coffee shops, and other spots where friends meet to discuss their lives are good areas to see the yadda yadda yadda gesture in use, though, as mentioned above, it is not used as frequently these days as it was a few years ago.

Execution: 1. Raise one arm to about neck level.

              2. Splay your fingers outward.

              3. Twirl your hand in a circle several times.

              4. This gesture may be punctuated by saying "Yadda yadda yadda."

Variations of   See BLAH BLAH BLAH, page 185.
Performance:

VII. No Words Needed

88. 📷 **BLAH BLAH BLAH**

Usage and Origins:

The fingers of one hand are held straight and stiff, with the tips touching the thumb and flapping up and down as if inside a puppet. The blah blah blah gesture mimes the action of talking, with the fingers and thumb representing the movement of a jaw going up and down. A person who flashes this gesture is imitating a person who talks too much, gossips, or is boring.

This is a signal that may be shown to the person who is talking incessantly, though it may also be done behind his back or to indicate that another person who is not present is the blabbermouth.

It may also be used to skip over some part of a story that is being related, as in, "It was a fun night. We went out, blah blah blah, I'm really hung over this morning." (see YADDA YADDA YADDA, page 182).

Region:

This gesture is most common in the United States and other parts of the Western world.

Environment:

You will see this gesture virtually anywhere, as boredom is not site-specific. Some likely locales are the workplace (in the midst of a long meeting) or a lecture hall (when a professor seems to enjoy the sound of his own voice).

Parties, bars, restaurants, and other areas where tales may go on too long are good spots to use the blah blah blah gesture.

Execution:
1. **Raise your hand level with your shoulder, but at a comfortable distance from it.**

2. **Show the hand, palm out, with fingers held together.**

3. **Bring the fingers down to meet the thumb, then back up again** [Fig. A].

4. **Repeat step 3 several times.**

Fig. A

Variations of Performance:
In Italy, only the forefinger and middle fingers are used to indicate that a windbag is present.

89. 🔘 **CALL ME**

Usage and Origins:

The thumb and little finger are splayed out from a fist and held to the face, with the little finger near the mouth and the thumb near the ear, as if miming the shape of a telephone receiver. The meaning of this gesture can largely be defined by context. It is sometimes used at the end of a conversation; for example, when departing after a meeting or exchange, a person might flash the gesture as a reminder for the other party to keep in touch.

Slightly less commonly, this gesture may mean "You have a phone call." For bold flirters, this entreaty to contact the gesturer may be used when no words have been spoken between the two in the exchange.

Though at one time it was used semi-seriously, today this gesture has become such a part of the gestural lexicon that it is often exercised tongue-in-cheek. Sarcastic gesturers pretend to be Valley girls or harried businessmen, two stereotypical characters who abuse the gesture.

You may take the flirtatious performance of this gesture facetiously if it is executed with an excess of smarminess. (Do not confuse the call me gesture with HANG LOOSE [see page 13] or LET'S DRINK [see page 213], which have very similar hand positions; for those gestures, the hands are held at different areas of the body.)

Region: This gesture will likely be understood in any area of the world where phone usage is prevalent, even if it is not part of the national lexicon. Due to the variations in meaning, be careful to clarify through performance whether flirtation is intended.

Environment: A busy street corner, outside a corporate conference room, or across a crowded room are common spots where this gesture is put to good use.

Along with the gesture's execution, the environment in which it is performed is a good way to surmise the intent of the gesturer; when seen in a dimly-lit bar, perhaps across empty bottles and glasses, this gesture will have a different significance than when your mother motions to you from the window as you pull out of the driveway.

Execution: 1. **Make a fist with one hand** [Fig. A].

2. **Extend your thumb and pinkie** [Fig. B].

3. **Raise your hand and place your knuckles along your chin, orienting your pinkie near your mouth and your thumb near your ear** [Fig. C].

4. **Twist your wrist from side to side. Your pinkie and thumb should trace out small arcs in the air approximately one inch wide.**

5. Simultaneously raise both eyebrows in a questioning way.

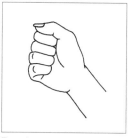

Fig. A

Fig. B

Fig. C

| Variations of Performance: | Though this gesture is performed fairly uniformly regardless of meaning, there are ways to strengthen the intent of "call me." The raising of the eyebrows might turn into a suggestive wiggle, or the eyebrow- |

raise might be eliminated altogether, depending on the seriousness of the setting. You may add the sound of a ringing phone to the performance of the gesture to further drive home the point.

In Argentina, one signals to someone that he is wanted on the phone by making a gesture similar to the American symbol for CRAZY (see page 196); the index finger is used to trace a circle around the ear, imitating the action of holding an early, now mostly outdated, version of the telephone receiver to the ear.

90.   📷   **CHECK PLEASE**

Usage and Origins:

The thumb and index finger form a ring while the other fingers remain slack; the hand is held in the air and mimes the action of writing. This gesture is used solely in restaurants, taverns, cafes, and other dining establishments to signal to a member of the waitstaff that you are ready to pay your bill and depart.

The check please gesture is a way to make your request known without shouting or leaving your table, and when a restaurant is busy or crowded, the gesture saves your server an extra trip to the table.

Region:

The check please gesture is used in North America and Western Europe.

Environment: As noted above, this gesture will seldom, if ever, be used outside of commercial eating establishments.

Execution:
1. Make eye contact with the waiter/waitress.

2. Raise your arm above your head.

3. Bring the tips of your index finger and thumb together and form a loose fist with your remaining fingers, as if holding a pencil.

4. Wiggle your hand up and down at the wrist to mimic writing [Fig. A].

5. Move your arm in the air from left to right approximately half a foot as you trace out your "signature." It does not matter if you intend to pay with cash.

Fig. A

Variations of
Performance:

Instead of miming the writing of a check you may simply make a checkmark in the air to let a waiter know you would like to settle up [Fig. B]. Likewise, you may keep your arm down near the table instead of up in the air while performing the main execution of the gesture.

In Mexico, you might call the server over by making kissing noises (see Kɪss Kɪss, page 97). Finally, in the finest restaurants and with the best service, all you will need to do is make eye contact, and your server will know what you need.

Fɪɢ. B

91. 📷   **COME HERE**

Usage and
Origins:

The palm is held face up, and the index finger is crooked toward the body. The use of this gesture makes it possible to call a person over wordlessly, which can be advantageous in a crowded setting or when one wants to be seductive. The symbolic pulling of someone toward you can be simply utilitarian, as in "Come here, I need to talk to you," or it may be flirtatious, as in, "I like the look of you, and I'd like to get to know you better."

Region:

This is just one of many ways to say "come here" around the world. It is the primary gesture used for beckoning in the United States and most of Europe, including the British Isles, Scandinavia, Holland, Belgium, Germany, Austria, France, and the former Yugoslavia.

In Italy and Greece, the come here gesture using the whole hand is very similar to a "goodbye wave" (see WAVING, page 32), which can certainly be confusing—it's the exact opposite of a beckon! In Malaysia and the former Yugoslavia, use the finger beckon to call animals only; calling to a human in this way is considered rude. In Indonesia and Australia, the fingertip beckon is reserved for calling to prostitutes.

Environment: Parties are perhaps the most common locale for see-
ing the come here gesture employed, as they are often
both crowded and good places to flirt. Other common
spots to see this signal flashed are bars, which may
also be densely populated with attractive people.

Execution: 1. Hold your hand out in front of your body.
Either crook your arm at the elbow or extend
your arm fully.

2. Orient your hand so that it is horizontal, palm
up.

3. Curl your index finger up and around until it is
pointing back toward your body. It will sweep in
an arc [Fig. A].

4. Uncurl your finger until your hand is flat once
again [Fig. B].

5. Repeat as needed.

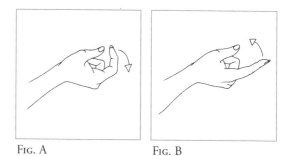

Fig. A   Fig. B

| Variations of Performance: | In many regions of the world, such as Italy, Spain, Portugal, Greece, Malta, Tunisia, Turkey, and parts of Asia, Africa, and South America, the come here gesture is practiced upside-down, with the fingers sweeping under. This looks very much like the northern European "go away" gesture, which can be the source of much confusion (See GET OUT, page 203). |

The hand beckon, with the palm held up and all the fingers curled up in a repeated motion, is used with the same meaning.

92. 📷 **CRAZY**

Usage and
Origins:

The index finger of one hand traces a circle near the temple. In the performance of this gesture, the movement of the finger symbolizes a loose brain rolling around. The crazy gesture is employed to indicate that you or another person is not mentally sound; this is not a clinical designation but a flippant way to describe someone who is irrational or simply "out there."

In most regions, it doesn't matter which direction the finger is turned—it may be clockwise or counterclockwise. However, in Japan, the crazy gesture must be enacted counterclockwise, as if winding a clock in the wrong direction. This is called *Hidarimaki*, or "to wind counterclockwise"; if the finger moves in a clockwise direction, it means "vain." The distinction between the directions is an old tradition that is fast fading away as new generations come of age; both directions are coming to mean crazy in Japan.

Region:

This gesture is understood throughout the world to mean crazy, though around the globe there are many other ways to imply that a person is not all there.

In Argentina, this gesture can be used to let someone know he has a phone call, as it is the mime of holding an old-fashioned telephone receiver to the ear.

Environment: The crazy gesture may be invoked most anywhere to assert that a person is irrational or just plain batty; from the workplace to happy hour at a neighborhood watering hole to the Laundromat, crazy people, and therefore the gesture, abound.

Execution:
1. **Make a fist with one hand** [FIG. A].

2. **Extend your index finger** [FIG. B].

3. **Raise your arm to point at your temple, but do not touch it.**

4. **Slowly rotate the finger, mapping a small circle to the side of your temple** [FIG. C].

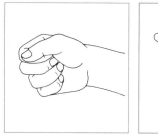

FIG. A

FIG. B

Fig. C

Variations of
Performance:

In the Western world, using an index finger to mime a screwdriver drilling into the temple means "He has a screw loose," or "He is not quite right in the head." Similarly, in Southern Italy, the thumb and index finger are twisted at the temple to mime the action of tightening a loose screw.

Finally, all over the world you will find the temple tap—wherein the index finger taps the temple—to mean one of two things: That a person is crazy or that she is really smart. Context will help in divining the specific meaning.

93. 📷 **DUH!**

Usage and Origins:

The heel of the hand slaps the forehead. In the performance of this gesture, your own hand acts like the hand of another, slapping your forehead in order to illustrate that you've said or done something untoward or unintelligent.

You may also slap your own forehead and say "Duh!" as a way to let another know that he has said or done something silly or inappropriate. This gesture is enacted when you forget something or remember something, such as where you left your keys or an answer on an already-taken examination, and will be used the same way whether it is the loss or the retrieval being accentuated.

Region:

The duh! gesture is widespread but is most commonly used in the United States, as well as in central and eastern Europe.

Environment:

Since people say and do silly or inappropriate things most anywhere, this gesture will not be limited to any specific locations. However, the duh! gesture will see an increased usage in classrooms during tests, quizzes, and exams of all kinds as students puzzle over the answers to tricky questions.

Execution: 1. **Open your hand so that your palm is facing your head.**

2. **Slap the heel of your palm against your forehead.**

3. **You may say "Duh!" for extra emphasis.**

Variations of   For added emphasis, you may actually lightly slap the
Performance: forehead of another if you believe he has done something worthy of the duh! gesture, though undue
violence ought to be avoided.

94.   **FINGERS CROSSED**

Usage and   *The index and middle fingers of one hand are crossed,*
Origins: *with the middle finger being brought over top of the*
index finger. When a person displays the fingers crossed
gesture, one of two major meanings are possible. One
idea expressed by the fingers crossed gesture is good
luck. The other main meaning of the crossed fingers
gesture refers to the relationship between two people,
with the fingers themselves being representative of
two people in a close friendship, whether it is romantic
or platonic.

As a good luck or protection symbol, experts
believe this gesture most likely has its roots as a mod-
ified Christian sign of the cross. Over the years, the

Christian meaning has been obscured and forgotten, largely because the crossed fingers gesture looks nothing like the crucifixion.

These days, the crossing of the fingers is more of a superstitious, secular gesture and may be used to wish a friend luck, as in "I'm keeping my fingers crossed for you," or as a luck symbol for oneself. Children are a big proponent of this gesture, though they usually use it when telling white lies, believing that having the fingers crossed makes it okay to fib. Again, this belief may have its origin in Christian crucifix symbolism; calling on the power of the cross might save one from being sent to hell for telling a lie.

When using the fingers crossed gesture to refer to a relationship, it will generally be accompanied by the phrase "We're like this," "They're like this," or the like. Taking this meaning one step further, the fingers can be symbolic of two people in the act of copulation to refer to a sexual relationship, though this meaning is much less common.

In southern Italy, Turkey, and other Mediterranean countries, after two friends argue one might cross his fingers and put them in the face of the other. The symbolic end of the friendship occurs when one or the other of the two pulls the fingers apart.

Region: As a gesture of good luck, you'll witness the fingers crossed gesture in historically Christian countries, most commonly in the United States, United Kingdom, and Scandinavia.

As an indicator of a close relationship, this gesture is used the world over.

Environment: The crossed fingers gesture will be used to wish good luck to another in such varied settings as sports fields, doctor's offices, and backstage at theaters. Since luck is beneficial in most of life's arenas, you will see this gesture most anywhere.

This is true of the friendship usage of the crossed fingers, too; close relationships are discussed and cemented everywhere, from the supermarket to the golf course to your own living room.

Execution: 1. **Make a loose fist with one hand.**

2. **Extend your index and middle fingers.**

3. **Cross the extended fingers, generally with the middle finger over the index finger.**

4. **Shake the entire hand.**

Variations of Performance: You may cross the fingers of both hands for "extra" luck. Children often suggest that they will keep all of their fingers and toes crossed in hopes of more luck; this is impossible, however heroic the effort.

95. 📷 **GET OUT!**

Usage and
Origins:

The hand shoos away unwanted pests or people by flicking back and forth at the wrist, imitating the action of a broom. The get out! gesture mimes the action of pushing something unwanted away and is used to let a person or an animal know that he is unwanted on the premises. Seriously shooing a person out of an area is extremely rude and is therefore not often done in a malicious way; in fact, it is generally done in a joking context or at a time when one simply doesn't want another person to see what she is doing, such as wrapping his birthday gift.

The get out! gesture is more likely to be done in earnest in reaction to a pest that is where it shouldn't be—a bee in the house, seagulls swarming at the beach, the neighbor's cat in your garden. You may also use this gesture with your own dog or cat when it finds its way into your closet, refrigerator, desk drawer, or anywhere else it could cause trouble or irritation.

Region:

The get out! gesture is used just about everywhere. In Spain, Portugal, Italy, Malta, Tunisia, Greece, and Turkey, this can be a very confusing gesture, however: In these countries, a very similar signal means, "come here," so this gesture doubles as a beckoning and a shooing gesture (see COME HERE, page 193).

Environment: Grooms in Western countries see this gesture on their wedding day: Bridesmaids try to ensure that the groom doesn't see the bride in her gown before she walks down the aisle. Other common spots to see this gesture include hiding spots for holiday gifts and anywhere insects or animals are unwanted.

Execution: 1. **Hold out your arm in front of you.**

    2. **Orient your hand so that your fingers point down, with your palm facing your body.**

    3. **Flick your hand away from your body at the wrist.**

    4. **Repeat.**

Variations of Performance: You may use both hands at once.

96.   **GUN TO HEAD**

Usage and Origins: *The thumb and index finger are extended, with the thumb pointing upward and the tip of the index finger touching the temple, imitating a pistol held to the head.* The gun to head gesture implies suicide, meaning one of four things: "I'm so stupid for saying that, I could just shoot myself"; "I shot myself in the head by saying that—now I'll never get the job"; "I had to do it—he had a gun to my head"; or, least commonly, "I'd rather be dead than engage in this activity any longer."

It is important to note that this gesture is almost always done in jest; the gesturer rarely, if ever, will actually be indicating that he is going to shoot himself in the head.

Region: This gesture enjoys popular usage in the United States, as well as regions where American culture has permeated.

Environment: Since people tend to say untoward things and then feel badly about it or become desperately bored just about everywhere, this gesture will be seen in a wide variety of locales, from first-date hot-spots and lecture halls to office buildings and movie theaters.

Execution: 1. Make a fist with one hand.

2. Extend the thumb and index fingers.

3. Bring the hand up to your head, resting the tip of your index finger against your temple with your thumb pointing up in the air [Fig. A].

4. Jerk your index finger away from the head, pre-
    tending to shoot yourself.

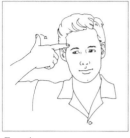

Fig. A

Variations of
Performance:

No matter what part of your head you point the
"gun" to, the idea of the gesture will be conveyed. To
exaggerate the gesture further, you may open your
mouth and put the "gun" in it or emit a "shooting"
noise when making the gesture.

97.   **HEAR NO EVIL**

Usage and
Origins:

The hands are cupped and held over the ears. The hear
no evil gesture is understood in several slightly different ways, but it is always a sign that the gesturer wants
a noise to cease. It may be an almost unconscious
action, as when a fire truck blaring its siren drives by

your house or a car alarm honks endlessly. It may sometimes be used deliberately, in order to block out something that is being said.

Children often employ this gesture to let parents know that what they are saying is unpleasant or unwarranted. This is more of a symbolic blockage of sound, since simply cupping the hands over the ears only mutes it, but it certainly gets the message across.

You may use the gesture to signal to a roommate to turn down loud music or to a chatterbox friend to let him know you'd prefer silence to his incessant yakking.

Region: The hear no evil gesture is utilized worldwide to mute unwanted noise.

Environment: Children's bedrooms are popular spots to see this gesture, used by youngsters who'd rather not heed parents' commands.

Dormitories, loud bars and clubs, and city streets are common areas for people to clamp their hands defensively over their ears to block out sound.

Execution: 1. **Position one open hand over each of your ears.**

2. **Shake your head from side to side.**

Variations of
Performance:

The tips of the index fingers can be inserted into the ears to plug noise from getting through. This is more often used as a pointed form of the gesture, deliberately performed to get your "Turn it down" or "Stop making that noise" message across.

The gesture may also be accompanied by the words "I'm not listening to you" or by nonsense sounds, such as "la la la," to indicate that you aren't going to pay heed to what is said.

98. **HOT**

Usage and
Origins:

One open hand is shaken vigorously near the neck. This gesture has a number of different specific meanings, but all are concerned in some way or another with oneself, someone else, or something being "hot."

The action of the gesture mimes a fan flapping to cool the face and neck. The first meaning is literal; you may use your hand to fan yourself when it is too hot. The hand-fan doesn't necessarily cool you down, but it does provide the illusion of cool air coming in contact with your body.

Similarly, you may use the hot gesture to describe a man or woman you find particularly attractive, as is done with The Sizzle (see page 100). The sentiment here is that a person is so hot, or arousing, that you perform the gesture to symbolically cool yourself down. You may make this gesture directly to the attractive person or use it when talking about that person to someone else.

Finally, the hot gesture is used to indicate that you've gotten through a situation over whose outcome you were sweating. It was a close call, but you escaped without harm or adverse effects coming to you.

Region: Each of the three meanings of this gesture will be implied with its use the world over; context will elucidate which sentiment is being indicated.

Environment: At the gym or on the beach or patio are good places to see this gesture used to indicate literal heat. These areas are also places one is likely to encounter attractive people, so that meaning of the gesture will be indicated in these spots; however, attractive people abound, so you'll see the hot gesture in use to describe and/or indicate arousal due to attraction most anywhere.

Likewise, close calls are abundant in life, so the hot gesture will be employed to indicate that a tight situation has been averted everywhere from your office to the doctor's office.

Execution: 1. **Raise your arm until your hand is at neck level.**

2. **Let your hand hang limply, fingers slightly apart.**

3. **Flap your hand vigorously at the wrist, shaking your hand** [Fig. A].

4. **If the subject is especially "hot," furrow your brow for emphasis, and whistle quietly.**

Fig. A

Variations of Performance:

You may perform this gesture directly in front of your mouth to indicate that a food or drink is either very spicy or very hot in temperature. Though this action will have little effect on the condition of your mouth, it will effectively warn a companion of the condition of the consumables.

In Japan, when the right hand, with the palm facing left, is fanned back and forth in front of the face, it assumes the meaning of the lateral head shake, or "no" (see Nod No, page 69).

99. 📷 **HUNGRY**

Usage and Origins:
One hand is rubbed in a circle on the abdomen. The hand rubbing the belly is a mime of an attempt to alleviate the pain caused by hunger. You may see children or adults doing this, signaling that it is lunch or dinner time, but the hungry gesture will rarely be used as an indication of anything more than slight hunger pangs; this gesture will not be used to describe malnutrition or starvation.

Region:
The hungry gesture is sometimes performed unconsciously and is used worldwide.

Be careful of contextal clues in Central Europe, where this same gesture can be insulting. In this case, rubbing the abdomen can mimic the action of soothing pain caused by too much belly-laughter; if a person flashes this gesture he's suggesting to you that he is happy about your bad luck and has been laughing about your misfortune. You can tell the two gestures apart by looking at the movement of the hand: The hunger gesture is more circular, while the motion of the mean-spirited gesture is vertical.

Environment:
School cafeterias, restaurants, and your home's dining room are common spots to see this gesture enacted to convey peckishness. Hunger can strike when food is not near, however, so also look for this gesture in

classrooms, while shopping at the mall, or while hiking through the forest.

Execution:

1. **Place one hand on your abdomen.**

2. **While touching your stomach, move your hand in a circular movement.**

3. **Repeat several times.**

Variations of Performance:

To indicate extreme hunger, the stomach clasp is a popular universal alternative to the hungry gesture. In this variation, the hand grabs the stomach as opposed to rubbing it.

In Greece, the stomach "saw" is a variation wherein your hand performs a palm-up sawing motion rather than a clasping one. A similar variation can be found in Italy, where the stomach is "cut" with the side of a flat hand, palm-down, in a rhythmic motion across the abdomen.

In Latin America, hunger is indicated by pressing the sides of the stomach with both hands and opening the mouth, mimicking the pain of starvation.

100. 📷 **LET'S DRINK**

Usage and Origins:

The thumb and pinkie splay out from a fist and tilt back and forth at the wrist, with the tip of the thumb touching the lips. This gesture poses the question: "Would you like to get a drink?" It may also mean "I'm thirsty" and derives from miming the action of drinking from a canteen-type flask by squirting liquid into the mouth, as is common in Spain and the Middle East.

In most of the rest of the world, the gesture means the same thing, and it mimics the action of drinking from a cup or glass (see next page for full description of variations).

Region:

The let's drink gesture is beverage-oriented in most of the world, most notably in Spain, Spanish-speaking South America, and Arab nations.

Environment:

Around 5 P.M. at office buildings, you are likely to see the let's drink gesture used in excess. Likewise, bars and other drinking establishments are good places to see this gesture employed to suggest another round of beverages. Deserts and other places where water is scarce might see this gesture in use to connote thirst.

Execution:

1. Make a fist with one hand [FIG. A].

2. Extend your pinkie and thumb [FIG. B].

3. Bring your hand near your mouth in the air in front of your face, with your thumb near to your mouth.

4. Tip your hand back and forth, as if pouring liquid out of a bottle and into your mouth [FIG. C].

FIG. A

FIG. B

Fig. C

Variations of Performance:	If the hand is rotated from side to side, this gesture implies that someone is drunk and unable to keep the bottle straight.

In France, someone else's drunkenness can be gestured about by forming a ring with the index and forefingers, placing them around the nose, and then twisting the hand in a circular motion.

In most countries where the let's drink gesture is not seen, "I'm thirsty" or an invitation to drink is implied when a gesturer cups the hand as though it is holding an imaginary cup or glass and raises it to the lips. This version originated in the British Isles and spread around the world from there; it is now common in almost every culture where imbibing is done from a glass.

In Poland, a common, though fairly intimate, gesture of invitation to drink is a flick of a finger against the gesturer's neck. Beware: This gesture is conventional only among close friends and may be considered rude if performed for someone with whom one is not close.

---

101. 📷 **PREGNANT**

Usage and Origins:

The hand is arced over the stomach, tracing the curve of an imaginary swelled belly. This gesture, which indicates pregnancy, is performed by women and men alike and can be done without regard to whether the woman who is being referred to is actually swollen or even whether she is really pregnant.

Often, the gesture is used as a gossiping tool, and since gossip can be ill-informed, this indication of pregnancy should not be taken as gospel. This gesture will often be used as a way to indicate pregnancy without words—saying that a woman is pregnant can be uncomfortable, whether because she is not ready to discuss it or the gesturer believes that bad choices led to an unwanted pregnancy.

Region:

Due to the illustrative nature of the pregnant gesture, it will be understood almost everywhere. It is very commonly used in Lebanon, Jordan, and Syria.

Environment: Since the state of being pregnant is perennial, this gesture will be seen everywhere from doctors' offices to Babies "R" Us.

Similarly, since gossip knows no location, you'll see this gesture anywhere people congregate to share secrets, from restrooms to office buildings.

Execution: 1.   Open one hand so that it is flat.

2.   Position the open hand with your thumb touching the top of your belly, so your palm faces downward and is perpendicular to your body.

3.   Arc your hand over your stomach area, to imitate the curve of a pregnant belly [FIG. A].

4.   End with your hand facing upward, your pinkie touching your body at the bottom of your belly.

FIG. A

Variations of
Performance:

In Southern Italy, the clothing is pulled out and away from the body in the region near the abdomen, suggesting a pregnant belly.

102. 📷 **SAY WHAT?**

Usage and
Origins:

The hand is cupped around the ear. This gesture serves a dual purpose: Not only does cupping the ear let another person know, without words, that you are having a hard time hearing him and that he should speak up, the say what? gesture also helps you hear better. The cupping of the lobe makes the dish of the ear larger so that it is able to pull in more sound.

When performing the say what? gesture, you need only hold your hand at your ear for a moment, unless you are striving to hear something and have not yet heard it.

Region:

This gesture is employed the world over, both as an amplifying device and as an indicator that another should speak up.

Environment:

You might see the say what? gesture at a playhouse when the actors' microphones are not working properly or at an old movie theater where the sound is of poor quality. Lectures and rallies are popular spots to see this gesture employed, as public speakers often have difficulty projecting their voices. Crowded and noisy public places such as parades, taverns, and busy streets will see increased incidence of the say what? gesture.

Execution: 1. **Raise one hand level with your head.**

2. **Bring your hand to your ear.**

3. **Cup your hand around your ear.**

4. **Incline your head in the direction of what you are attempting to hear.**

103.   **SMOKING**

Usage and Origins:

The index and middle finger, held slightly apart, tap the lips repeatedly. This gesture is a simple mime of the action of smoking a cigarette and can be both a way to inquire if another will give you a cigarette and an invitation to another to join you for a smoke.

In some areas, be cautious when using the smoking gesture; due to its similarity to the "V" gesture (see page 227), it may be confused with a number of other implications. Be particularly wary in Britain, where the "V" is an insulting gesture.

Region: The smoking gesture is used worldwide, though you won't see it among non-smokers of any culture.

Environment: Public places where cigarette smoking is still allowed will see this gesture most often; bars, restaurants, and coffee houses will be the best places to view it. Street corners or outside of office buildings, where smokers often take their breaks, is another area where this gesture enjoys increased usage.

You may ask another to join you for a cigarette just about anywhere, whether you may smoke in that locality or must venture outside or to the bar to enjoy a shared smoke.

Execution: 1. **Make a loose fist with one hand.**

2. **Extend the index and middle fingers. They may be touching each other or slightly apart.**

3. **Place your index and middle fingers to your lips, either just touching them or almost touching them.**

4. **Move your fingers to about two inches from your lips, then quickly back to your lips.**

5. **Repeat this motion a few times.**

104. 📷 **STOP**

Usage and
Origins:

The body is positioned in a strong stance, with the feet slightly apart and the shoulders straight, while the arm is raised perpendicular to the ground and the hand is displayed palm-out. One of the simplest signs, the stop gesture is easily understood. The physical barrier it creates symbolically blocks a person from what she is doing, and she should understand that you would like her to cease.

The stop gesture is ancient in origin, with mentions in literature as far back as ancient Roman texts. Since the stop gesture employs a defensive stance, it may be used to stop a person from entering some space or may be intended as a warning that someone ought to stop pursuing a certain line of conversation.

Region:

The stop gesture is used worldwide with one important exception. Greece has is a similar-looking gesture with a different meaning: Thrusting the palm of the hand toward another is used to mean "Go to hell." Called the *Moutza*, this meaning has its origins in the ancient Byzantine Empire, when crimes were punished by chaining people and displaying them in the streets. There, locals would pick up dirt or excrement from the ground and rub it in the faces of the criminals with their open palms.

This ancient context is no longer part of popular usage; instead, the gesture has taken on new meaning, with each of the five fingers of the palm representing a different sexual act that the gesturer will perform on the sister of the person being gestured to. This is a popular gesture flashed in traffic jams and during other busy driving conditions, much like THE FINGER (see page 117) in the United States.

Environment: Since police use this gesture when directing traffic, good places to witness it are a crowded intersection or construction area. Often, the stop gesture is employed at parties to bar the entrance of undesirables.

Anywhere a conversation begins to veer in an uncomfortable direction, a person might employ this gesture to save others—as well as herself—from embarrassment.

Execution: 1. **Stand firmly with your legs spread shoulder width apart.**

2. **Extend an arm straight out in front of you.**

3. **Raise your hand at the wrist so that your hand is perpendicular to your arm, palm out.**

4. **Place your other hand on your hip to strike a more imposing figure.**

Variations of Performance: You may perform this gesture while seated, using just the raised hand. This variation will generally be used only during conversation and not as a physical barrier.

105. **TIME OUT**

Usage and Origins: *Both hands are held flat, with one hand situated horizontally and the fingertips of the other touching it at a 90-degree angle to form a "T."* The time out gesture originated in American football: The "T" formation stands for time out, a break to rest or discuss strategy.

This gesture has permeated social arenas, too. One might flash the time out gesture during an argument between two friends in order to try to calm them down or during a conversation when one needs a break. This may be done so that a participant can use the restroom, or simply to take a moment for a breather or to figure out what is being discussed.

Region: This gesture will still be most commonly seen in the United States but is spreading rapidly to all cultures.

Environment: A football or basketball game is still the best spot to view this gesture. There are other locales where the time out gesture will enjoy increased usage, such as dormitories, where arguments between friends abound due to close proximity and constant togetherness.

In bars and at parties, where alcohol flows copiously and confusion may result, people often use this gesture to take a rest from a complicated conversation.

Execution: 1. **Make loose paddles with both hands.**

2. **Bend your arms at the elbow to bring your hands to chest level.**

3. **Place the fingertips of your right hand against the palm of your left hand at a perpendicular angle to form a "T."**

4. **Release.**

Variations of Performance:
In Peru, the index finger instead of the whole hand forms the 90-degree angle against the horizontal palm, and this is usually employed in the context of employment, as at the end of the working day. It is unclear whether this gesture arose independently of the American time out; some experts speculate that the horizontal palm mimes the action of how a worker will look once he gets home from work and lies down to relax.

In Italy, this same version of the gesture is used to call friends together to start a game or group activity.

106. 📷 **THUMB TWIDDLE**

Usage and Origins:
The hands are clasped together, with the thumbs rotating around each other repeatedly. The thumb twiddle is a gesture borne of boredom and impatience, and experts believe the action is akin to the pacing of a caged animal. They speculate that the gesture is performed because the person feels that doing something, even something so small, is better than doing nothing at all.

The thumb twiddle may be done solely for the benefit of oneself, or more commonly, it can be done as a deliberate display to another to show that one is not interested in what is occurring and would rather that it stopped.

Region:
The thumb twiddle gesture is employed by bored people around the globe.

Environment:
Boredom and impatience have a tendency to strike anywhere, though common spots to see individuals engaged in thumb-twiddling are waiting areas in hospitals, garages, the Division of Motor Vehicle Offices, while sitting in traffic, or during a truly mundane class or lecture.

Execution:

1. **Bring your hands together.**

2. **Interlock your fingers, except your thumbs [Figs. A and B].**

3. **Rotate your thumbs around one another [Fig. C].**

4. **Repeat several times or until boredom subsides.**

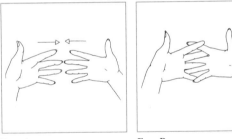

Fig. A

Fig. B

Fig. C

107. 📷 **THE "V"**

Usage and
Origins:

The index and middle fingers are splayed out from a fist to make a "V." The "V" gesture has multiple meanings that depend on whether the palm faces away from or toward the body. The "V" gesture with the palm out means victory.

Contrary to popular belief, Winston Churchill did not originate this gesture, though he did popularize it. Actually, a Belgian lawyer, appropriately named Victor De Lavelaye, set out to find a symbol that could be used for the international Nazi-resistance movement in the 1940s. The Belgian underground Nazi-resistance movement had been using the letters "R.A.F." to insult the Germans until that time. To avoid confusion internationally, and to find one gesture for all, De Lavelaye came up with the letter "V," since it fit not only the English word for "victory," but also the Flemish and the French.

On January 14, 1941, De Lavelaye was interviewed on a wartime broadcast, where he suggested that the "V" gesture be used in a large anti-Nazi propaganda campaign. The BBC immediately picked up on it; subsequently, Churchill began to use the sign, and it spread as a very well-known symbol for victory against Nazi oppression. This gesture's use has now broadened and permeated cultures worldwide.

Politicians can often be seen flashing this gesture

at political rallies, signifying their belief that their candidate will win. Richard Nixon was famous for flashing the double "V" gesture; the double "V" gesture was often used derisively against him in the post–Watergate era.

The palm-out "V" gesture is also used as a symbol of peace. American hippies took the "V" for "Victory" symbol and converted it into a more general "peace" sign that conveyed the hope that the war in Vietnam would end rather than be "won." The "V" gesture for peace was a sign of resistance to the police as well; hippies were able to take the insulting meaning of the gesture from Britain (see below), turn it around, and covertly put it into practice in the United States without fear of police retaliation. The palm-out version of the "peace" sign is still widely used, and in the United States this meaning is perhaps even better known than the original victory meaning.

With the palm facing toward the body, the "V" gesture translates roughly to mean "Up yours!" in Britain and British-influenced countries such as Ireland and Malta. The origin of this as an insulting gesture is unknown but highly speculated upon. One possibility is that during the Norman invasion, English archers were warned that if they lost their battles their first two fingers would be amputated, making it impossible for them to use their bows and arrows ever again. Therefore, when they won battles, they would flash their first two fingers at the defeated French to taunt them.

Other possible origins of the gesture include a badly made horns gesture (see page 160); an enlarged penis symbol; two penises; female genitals; fingers inserted into the vagina as foreplay; or a perversion of the Saudi Arabian "V" ON THE NOSE (see page 136).

Regardless of its origin, it will be read as extremely insulting, meaning "Fuck you" or "Up yours" and is used in much the same way as the American middle finger gesture (see page 117).

Region: As the symbol for "victory," the "V" gesture is understood around the world. The peaceful sentiments conveyed by this gesture will be felt in North America and other countries highly influenced by the American hippie counterculture of the 1960s and '70s.

Use this gesture to insult another in the British Isles and former British colonies that retain the Anglo influence, such as Malta.

Environment: The "V" gesture is perhaps the only gesture that unites politicians and protesters; you will see this symbol at both political establishments and counterculture activist rallies.

British pubs are popular spots to see the "V" gesture used insolently.

Execution: 1. **Make a fist with one hand.**

               2. **Extend your index and middle fingers.**

               3. **Spread your fingers apart to form a "V."**

---

108. 📷   **WHOOP-TEE-DO**

Usage and   *The forefinger of one hand is twirled about next to the*
Origins: *head.* The whoop-tee-do is a sarcastic gesture that
                signals annoyance or fake excitement. Flashing this
                gesture generally translates to "Who cares?" as in
                "She told me the play-by-play of her night, including
                what she ate—very exciting." The sarcastic "Big deal"
                may also be implied by this gesture, as in "My
                employer just gave me a raise—$200 more a year."

                The origin of this gesture is unknown, but the
                action of it could be an imitation of a noisemaker at
                a party. Regardless, apathetic teenagers, ironic 20-
                somethings, and any individuals who prefer to deal
                sarcastically with disappointment are the biggest pro-
                ponents of the whoop-tee-do gesture.

Region: This gesture is popular only in North America.

Environment: Office parties are a common spot to see the whoop-
                tee-do gesture in action, as are any spots where friends

gather to exchange tales of disappointment and mediocre activities.

Execution: 1. **Make a fist with one hand** [Fig. A].

2. **Extend the index finger** [Fig. B].

4. **Aiming your finger straight up, twirl your finger in the air beside your head** [Fig. C].

Fig. A

Fig. B

Fig. C

Sources

Axtell, Roger E. *Gestures: The Dos and Taboos of Body Language around the World*, rev. and expanded ed. New York: Wiley & Sons, 1998.

Bäuml, Betty J. and Franz H. Bäuml. *Dictionary of Worldwide Gestures*, 2d ed. Lanham, Md.: The Scarecrow Press, Inc., 1997.

Crawley, Mark. "Favorite Seinfeld Episodes: The Yada Yada." Movieprop.com [cited 15 September 2002]. Available from World Wide Web: (http://www.movieprop.com/tvandmovie/Seinfeld/favorite.htm)

"Death of an Icon." Rock and Roll Confidential 2002 [cited 15 September 2002]. Available from World Wide Web: (http://www.rockandrollconfidential.com/death.shtml).

Krazy George. "Krazy George Speaks on the Wave Controversy." Home page. 26 October 2001. [cited 27 August 2002]. Available from World Wide Web: (http://www.gameops.com/sro/krazy/_statement.htm).

Levine, Judith. "Crack Addiction: The Gentle Art of Mooning." *Nerve.com* 1999. [cited 11 September 2002]. Available from World Wide Web: (http://www.nerve.com/Dispatches/Levine/mooning/)

Ludowyk, Frederick. "Brass Razoo: Is It But a Breath of Wind?" *Ozwords* April 2000. Australian National Dictionary Centre, Australian National University [cited 28 August 2002]. Available from World Wide Web: (http://www.anu.edu.au/ANDC/Ozwords/April_2000/Brassrazoo.html).

Melanie and Mike. "Spotlight on Obscure Slang." *Take Our Word for It* 26 October 1998: 14. The Institute for Etymological Research and Education [cited 28 August 2002]. Available from World Wide Web: (http://www.takeourword.com/Issue014.html).

Morris, Desmond. Bodytalk: The Meaning of Human Gestures. New York: Crown Publishers Inc., 1994.

———. Manwatching: *A Field Guide to Human Behavior.* New York: Harry N. Abrams, Inc., 1977.

Morris, Desmond, Peter Collett, Peter Marsh, and Marie O'Shaughnessy. *Gestures: Their Origins and Distribution.* New York: Stein and Day, 1979.

Pingol, Kathleen. "Loser!" University of California Los Angeles Folklore & Mythology Archives [cited 15 September 2002]. Available from World Wide Web: (http://www.humnet.ucla.edu/humnet/folklore/folk15/Kathleen%20Pingol/Other/Loser.html).

———. "Whatever!" University of California Los Angeles Folklore & Mythology Archives [cited 15 September 2002]. Available from World Wide Web: (http://www.humnet.ucla.edu/humnet/folklore/folk15/Kathleen%20Pingol/Other/Whatever.html).

The University of Washington Husky Marching Band. "History: 1960–1989." [cited 27 August 2002]. Available from World Wide Web: (http://depts.washington.edu/hmb/thehmb/history4.shtml).

Welin, Chris. "Making Waves Over the Cheer." *The Dallas Morning News*, 15 November 1984. Gameops.com [cited 27 August 2002]. Available from World Wide Web: (http://www.gameops.com/sro/krazy/_dallas.htm).

Wheeler, Grady and Jon Cudo. "A Wave of Controversy." 2001: Gameops.com. [cited 27 August 2002]. Available from World Wide Web: (http://www.gameops.com/assets/pdf/wave.pdf).

Index

Numbers in **bold** (for example, **23**) are gesture numbers, and can be used to locate gestures in the photograph section. All other numbers are page numbers.